CHRIST WITH US

CHRIST WITH US

Roy Lawrence

Scripture Union

Scripture Union, 207–209 Queensway, Bletchley, MK2 2EB, England.

© Roy Lawrence 1997

First published 1997

ISBN 1 85999 201 3

The right of Roy Lawrence to be identified as author of this work has been asserted by him in accordance with the Copyright, Designs and Patents Act 1988.

Unless otherwise attributed, scripture quotations are taken from the Holy Bible, New International Version. Copyright © 1973, 1978, 1984 by International Bible Society. Anglicisation copyright © 1979, 1984, 1989. Used by permission of Hodder and Stoughton Limited.

British Library Cataloguing-in-Publication Data
A catalogue record for this book is available from the British Library.

Cover design by ie Design.
Cover illustration by Rosemary Woods.

Printed and bound in Great Britain by Cox & Wyman Ltd, Reading.

*My wife and I gratefully dedicate this book
to our sons, our daughters-in-law, our grandchildren
and to all our wider family.
Christ be with us all.*

CONTENTS

•

NB The stories in this book are all based on real events. But, in order to preserve anonymity, most of the names and a few of the details have been changed.

Chapter 1

IN OUR EARLY YEARS

We tend to take it so casually, don't we, the concept of the Christ who is with us? It is a truly amazing doctrine, unparalleled in the religions and philosophies of this world. Yet if familiarity has not exactly bred contempt, it has certainly dulled our sense of wonder. We only have to think of Christmas cards with their pictures of an idealised baby in a sanitized stable, surrounded by cuddly animals, and the feeling that comes across is probably one of warm sentimentality. In fact this feeling, if we stop to think about it, is inadequate almost to the point of blasphemy!

When I am told that God became man, I can follow the idea, but I just do not understand what it means. For what man, if left to his natural promptings, if he were God, would humble himself to lie in the feedbox of a donkey or to hang upon a cross? God laid upon Christ the iniquity of us all. That is that ineffable and infinite mercy of God which the slender capacity of man's heart cannot comprehend

and much less utter – that unfathomable depth and
burning zeal of God's love towards us.

Martin Luther

This book is an attempt to rediscover the sense of wonder
that Martin Luther and all great Christians have felt so
deeply throughout the centuries, and perhaps to uncover
something of the scandal of God's incarnation in a sinful
world. It is an attempt to rediscover this scandalous wonder
both in terms of personal belief and also in terms of life and
experience. Because if the Christian claims about Jesus are
true, they must make a radical difference to those who
receive them.

Later we will be looking at the actual historical process
which forms the basis of the Christian claim that Christ is
with us, the miracle of miracles without which it would be
impossible for us to be Christians today. Tentatively we will
attempt to discover some of the truths about the nature of
God and the destiny of man which are implicit within this
miracle. It will tax our tiny minds and our stunted souls to
their limits. At any rate it will tax mine! These concepts are
too big for us, but we must claim the privilege of making
the effort. It is part of the process of loving God with mind
and soul, which Jesus' first commandment lays upon us
(Mark 12:30). But before we lift our eyes to those theological horizons, I want to focus on something that is much
more earthy.

When theologians describe Christianity as an 'incarna-
tional' religion, one of the things they are saying is that
being a Christian is essentially a 'down-to-earth' experience. Jesus makes a difference to every stage in human life
in the here and now. And once the concept of 'Christ with
us' becomes a personal reality to any human being, nothing
can ever be quite the same again.

What I propose now is that we make a journey together through the different stages of life, looking into each for the practical implications of believing that Christ is with us. As we do so, I will draw on my own experiences and on those others have shared with me over the years, and I invite you to make this book a do-it-yourself experience. Not all of it will be true for you, but some aspects will apply directly and some will act as a mental springboard, a stimulus for your own very personal thoughts.

So let's begin at the beginning, contact the child inside ourselves and ask what difference it makes to start life with the assurance of Jesus' presence.

My mother and father were not regular churchgoers and their Christianity was distinctly vague. But I will always be grateful to them for teaching me that Jesus was with me at all times. I was a fairly nervous child: when the lights went out at night, I could not help imagining that there might just be something rather horrid under the bed and that if I put a bare foot to the floor I risked being gripped by a tentacle or nipped by sharp teeth. Of course, I knew with my conscious mind that there was nothing there in the darkness which had not been present in the light. But it was a greatly comforting thought that Jesus was right there with me, and that his love and his strength could more than make up for my fears and fantasies.

In our present parish church there is a lovely tapestry of Jesus as the Good Shepherd, surrounded by grazing sheep and holding a lamb in his arms. As a child I saw similar pictures and, though I would never have admitted it to any of my friends, I sometimes used to picture myself taking the place of the lamb in Jesus' arms. I was not aware that this is a properly biblical thing for Christians to do, but I did know that it gave me a good, safe feeling.

One of my former parishioners, Emily, did something

similar for her little granddaughter, Gemma. Gemma's sur-
name is Hogg and some of the children at her school were
giving her a hard time because of it. She cried as she told
her grandmother that they had nicknamed her 'Piggy' and
made 'oink, oink' noises whenever she walked by.

With great wisdom Emily said, 'They're only showing
their ignorance, my love.' And she took her dictionary down
off the shelf and read out its definition of a 'hogg' which is
not a pig but 'a young sheep that has not yet been sheared'.

'You're not a pig,' she said. 'You're a little lamb, and
you're safe in the arms of Jesus.'

Next day Gemma imperiously told her tormentors that
they were only showing their ignorance. She never had any
trouble again.

There can be no firmer foundation for life than the
knowledge of the loving Christ who is with us night and
day. In his book *To Define True Madness*, Dr Henry
Yellowlees writes, 'The greatest psychological asset any
human being can possess is a sense of confidence in his
environment – of trust in the strange incomprehensible
world into which he has mysteriously come and from which
he will as mysteriously depart.' The knowledge of Jesus'
presence brings this asset with it. Not only is the Christ who
is with us loving and strong, he is also at one with the heart
of cosmic reality, one with the Creator Father (John 10:30).
So it is wonderful to be able to sing with Anna Warner:

> Jesus loves me! This I know,
> For the Bible tells me so.
> Little ones to him belong;
> They are weak, but he is strong.

I remember the sense of shock I felt some years ago when I
heard a young man (whom I subsequently learned was a

Jehovah's Witness) question Jesus' love for children. We were at a wedding reception, and I was in the process of handing a 'Jesus loves me' sticker to a little girl who was also a guest. He came up to me and demanded what right I had to give it to her.

'How do you know he loves her?' he asked.

'He loves us all,' I said.

'Oh no, he doesn't,' he retorted as he turned on his heel and left us.

So *how* do I know that Jesus loves you and me and the little girl at the wedding reception? Well, Anna Warner was right – 'The Bible tells me so'. We need go no further than the famous account in Mark 10:13–16. It seems that Jesus had had a hard day. He was tired and the disciples were feeling protective towards him. So when people tried to bring little children to him to hold and bless, the disciples blocked the way.

Jesus reacted with positive indignation: 'Let the little children come to me, and do not hinder them, for the kingdom of God belongs to such as these. I tell you the truth, anyone who will not receive the kingdom of God like a little child will never enter it.' And, we are told, 'he took the children in his arms, put his hands on them and blessed them.' It is a gift beyond price to spend our childhood with the knowledge of those strong and saving hands around us.

Here then are three final thoughts before we turn our minds from the childhood years to those leading up to young adulthood.

I am convinced that Jesus has a particularly warm place in his heart for those who convey the gift of his presence to children. It is not easy to be a Christian teacher, or a leader of one of the Christian organisations for children, or even to be a Christian parent. So many pressures in our secular society militate against the Christian message. But there can be no greater gift than that of putting the hand of a child into the hand of Jesus. One of the great things about the move towards family/all-age services in the church is that it is inspired by the desire to bring that gift to all from the very earliest years. Not all churchgoers welcome these services as a part of their spiritual diet: they can seem noisy, casual and unstructured – though I know from experience they require more creative thought and detailed preparation than any other act of worship. But Jesus' command is as relevant and compelling now as it ever was: 'Let the little children come to me'.

Jesus adds a negative imperative: 'Do not hinder them'. We should grieve desperately for the many children who are denied the gift of the knowledge of Jesus' presence today. If this gift is denied out of ignorance, it is a tragedy. If it is denied not out of ignorance but as a deliberate act of choice, then it is more than a tragedy. It is an offence. And we know what Jesus says about those who offend against children. Here are his words as found in the bleak translation of the old King James' version of the Bible: '...woe unto him, through whom they [these offences] come! It were better for him that a millstone were hanged about his neck, and he cast into the sea, than that he should offend one of these little ones' (Luke 17:1–2).

You may, as you read this chapter, be aware of a sense of personal sadness or pain because of your own childhood experiences. It may be that you did not have the good fortune to know about Jesus in your earliest years. Or maybe no one made his love real to you. In fact, there may be stresses and horrors buried in your childhood which you do not even want to remember. The good news is that though you may not have known about Jesus he has always known about you, and even in life's worst moments he has never been far away – whether you were aware of him or not.

There is a spiritual process, sometimes known as 'the healing of memories', which allows Jesus to meet us at our points of inner deprivation and pain. May I illustrate this process by offering you a prayer exercise? It is in two parts. The first part is for us all. The second is just for those who need it.

Begin by reading again the story of Jesus blessing the children (Mark 10:13–16). However, this time allow yourself time to picture the scene. Jesus sitting by the wayside, the children managing to find their way to him (in spite of the disciples), the Lord's care, the Lord's embrace, the Lord's love, the Lord's blessing. In your imagination, picture yourself as a child among those children. Feel his arms around you. Rest and relax in his presence.

Then, if it is right and relevant in your case, you may feel able to go back in your mind to some painful childhood experience: but this time do not go alone – take Jesus with you. This process is a way to practise the Lord's presence in your own past. As you and he go back together, and you put the depths of your memory and the powers of your imagination at his disposal, what is he saying to you? What is he saying to any others who may be involved in your mental reconstruction of the scene? How is he affecting your understanding? Your pain? Your present involvement in past fears?

If it all becomes too much, you may need the help of a wise Christian friend or counsellor. If so, forget everything for now. Defer the act of recollection. Just concentrate on Jesus. But remember – there is nothing you and he cannot face together in the past, in the present, or in the future.[1] For the moment, let the apostle Paul offer us this perspective:

In all these things we are more than conquerors
through him who loved us. For I am convinced that

neither death nor life, neither angels nor demons,
neither the present nor the future, nor any powers,
neither height nor depth, nor anything else in all
creation, will be able to separate us from the love of
God that is in Christ Jesus our Lord.

Romans 8:37–39

Note

1 I have written at greater length about facing the pain,
the fear and the anger which so many of us have inside
ourselves in my book *How to Pray When Life Hurts*,
Scripture Union, 1993.

Chapter 2

GROWING UP

Young people have always been regarded with disquiet and suspicion by members of the older generation. If you can keep your eyes away from the third paragraph of this chapter, I wonder if you can guess who said the following and when:

> We are living in difficult and dangerous times. Youth
> has no regard for old age and the wisdom of
> centuries is looked upon by them as stupidity and
> foolishness. The young men are indolent and insolent
> and the young women are indecent and indecorous in
> their speech, their behaviour and their dress.

Answer: Peter the Hermit, in 1061!

Young people have often returned the compliment and had distinctly negative feelings about the older generation who they feel, with some justification, have made a mess of the world so far and are in no position to give lectures to anybody, least of all to those who will have to inherit the mess. As Rameses says to his father Seti, in *The Firstborn* by Christopher Fry, 'It's you who invite the future, but it's I who have to entertain it, remember that.'

Lord Reith must have rung a few bells when he said these words to the students of Glasgow University on the occasion of his installation as Rector: 'I warn you that you are going to find yourselves up against almost incredible inefficiency, incapacity, stupidity, unreliability, and indifference … The burden of what I am trying to say is – For God's sake, prevent it!'

However, I wonder whether he got as much response when he went on to add, 'Some definite and commanding confession, Christian or otherwise, is an integral part of life, the supreme factor for service, success and happiness.'

Personally, I am so glad and grateful that I found the Christian faith in a new and more committed way when I was a teenager – or rather, the Christian faith found me.

At the time I was at Manchester Grammar School and found myself sitting next to Peter who became a good friend. He invited me to visit him and his family during the school holidays, and it was then I discovered that his father was a curate, soon to be a vicar. When the family moved into their new home, they invited me to come and spend a week with them. I accepted, with a certain degree of apprehension. I was a non-churchgoer. How would I take to vicarage life? Would there be an oppressive religious atmosphere? Would I be got at?

I went with my defences well up, but this proved quite unnecessary. We had a great week and never once did they attempt to impose any religious views on me.

However, in spite of their restraint I became more and more aware that their house had something mine didn't, and I decided to find out what it was. When I was back home, on the following Sunday I surprised myself and my parents by going to the morning service in our local parish church. It was a disaster!

Not that there was much wrong with the service. The vicar was pleasant enough, and he preached quite a good sermon. It even contained a joke. It was the joke that was my downfall. I laughed out loud. It was obviously not the thing to do. A large and formidable lady sitting in front of me turned round and gave me a look that would have curdled fresh milk. After the service I made sure I spent a long time in prayer so she would be certain to leave well before me. All to no avail. As I opened my eyes she was still there, and she gave me a lecture I have never forgotten. It ended with these words: 'In future,' she boomed, 'model your behaviour on mine. I am always very reverent in church.'

It's amazing there was any future for me after this as far as the Church of England was concerned, but I did want to find out what it was that made such a difference to my friend's home. So I persevered in my Sunday morning churchgoing, though I kept well away from the large lady.

Following the worship was not always easy, and one Sunday I got totally lost in a sung Communion service. Afterwards I went to the vicar, whom I was now beginning to know, and asked for some help. He took me round to the vicarage and talked expansively on eucharistic theology.

'Does that answer your question?' he asked.

'No,' I replied. 'What I want to know is which page to turn to in the prayer book!'

I am grateful to have had this experience of the culture shock that so many go through when they first set foot in a church. I hope I have learned from it, because it can be a major factor in ensuring that non-churchgoers remain non-churchgoers. However, in my own case, in spite of these initial difficulties, I began to learn more about the Christian faith. I attended confirmation classes; I joined a lively

Christian youth club in a neighbouring parish. It gradually dawned on me that the heart of being a Christian lay in a personal relationship with Jesus and, in a bumbling way, only half-understanding what it was I was doing, I invited him into my life.

I was certainly going to need him. Those were the days of National Service and, at the age of seventeen, I found myself attached to the Highland Light Infantry, undergoing a fearsome course of army basic training at Fort George in the north of Scotland. You can hardly believe the shock to the system – I went from a home in which I was an only child and the apple of my mother's eye, from a school where I was a prefect and surrounded by the glow of having obtained a state scholarship to Oxford, to suddenly finding myself the lowest of the low in the army.

It was not just that I was initially one of the worst soldiers ever to put boot to parade ground, but my newly born Christian commitment was under continual attack. It was a world of profanity (I didn't even understand most of the swear-words that assaulted my eardrums), of pilfering (my first week's pay was stolen), and of sex without standards (more about this in the next chapter).

Anyone taking the Christian faith seriously seemed to have pathetic resources to pit against all this. Kenneth, an ordinand whom I met some time later, told me that he was persuaded by some of his fellow squaddies to go with them to a local brothel. They said it would broaden his experience and help to equip him for ministry, that he didn't need to do anything he didn't want to, he could just watch what was going on. But one of the women of the house came and sat on his knee, and began to arouse him. When she named a price and suggested he go with her to her room, he found he was powerless to resist. It was at that point he discovered his pocket had been picked. Since he had no money, his companion lost interest in him straightaway. Kenneth told me he has praised God for that pick-pocket every day since!

Unexpectedly, I was beginning to wonder whether I was being called to be an ordinand myself and I acquired the nickname of 'ministerrr' amongst the young Scots with whom I was training. It brought a stream of problems into my life. For instance, at the end of my very first day in the army I had to decide whether or not to kneel down by my bed in the barrack room to say my prayers. It would be so embarrassingly public, but I knew it was the right thing to do. So I took a deep breath and got down on my knees.

It was awful. Immediately I was surrounded by a group of squaddies, all having a great time at my expense. 'There are nae potties in the army, ministerrr,' they cackled, 'ye'll wet the floor!'

In time they got used to it. In fact, when someone came in from another squad and started to take the mickey out of me, they threw him out bodily. As the weeks went by, some even asked me to pray for them.

As my two years of National Service went by, I wish I could say my level of witness was always as good as that. The truth is, it was of a variable quality – sometimes good, sometimes not so good, sometimes non-existent. Life was a mixture of discoveries, difficulties, disasters and, occasionally, delights.

These days, of course, there is no National Service. Its tussles and trials are things of the past. However, I believe that the problems facing young people are greater than ever. Some of these are related to the increasing break-up of family life in a society where half our marriages now end in divorce or separation. Some stem from physical and emotional changes, which seem to take place earlier in life than they used to. Some are caused by unhealthy and unremitting media pressure. Some are the result of peer pressure in circles where the dangers range from the invasive drug culture to constant brand-name brainwashing. There are all kinds of pseudo solutions to life's problems, which focus attention primarily on the body and can produce side-effects such as anorexia nervosa and bulimia. Other new ingredients include the information super-highway which is both an opportunity and a danger, the rave scene with its hypnotic strobe lights and its (literally) deafening, thudding music, and the widespread rejection of traditional sexual restraints. I well remember the terrors of the assault course that was an obligatory part of National Service basic training. But this pales into insignificance beside the assault course built into young people's lives today.

It is a comfort that Christ does not come to us at this or any other stage of life to lecture or pontificate, though he has every right to do so. Incredibly, he comes to us as our peer, our equal. In Paul's words, Christ has 'emptied himself' of all the glory and privileges which are his by right as the Son of God:

> Who, being in very nature God,
>   did not consider equality with God something
>   to be grasped,
> but made himself nothing,
>   taking the very nature of a servant,
>   being made in human likeness.
> And being found in appearance as a man,
>   he humbled himself
>   and became obedient to death – even death on
>   a cross!

Philippians 2:6–8

In fact Paul seems to be saying that not only did Jesus come to us as our equal, but in a sense, he came as *less* than our equal!! In a world enmeshed by slavery, Jesus came as everybody's slave. He is our King but, as Graham Kendrick has put it, he is our 'Servant King' – never dominating, never pulling rank, never intimidating us from on high. And it is because, miraculously, he comes to us *from below*, no one need recoil from an initial encounter with him.

If we are fortunate enough to have that encounter in our teenage years, a rich and varied experience should lie ahead. He will still be the bringer of security, the Good Shepherd who holds each one of us like a lamb in his strong arms. And this is a very good experience to have, because the adolescent years are anxious years, whether we are prepared to show it or not. But Christ can be our role model, the embodiment of truth, and this is of particular importance at a stage of life when so much is baffling and bewildering.

Above all, the teenage years are a great time to discover Jesus as Saviour, the one who can rescue us from the evil around us and from the evil within us, and who has been prepared to pay an extraordinary price for doing so: 'he humbled himself and became obedient to death – even death on a cross'. We can have no more than a rudimentary understanding of this amazing truth when we are young, and indeed we will never fully fathom the wonder of it in this life. But, by the grace of God, we can find ourselves accepting Christ's saving act and marvelling at it, and begin to pick up clues about its meaning.

In the first parish in which I served as vicar we had a lively youth club. It was not always a safe place to be. Our policy was to admit everybody and occasionally there could be fist fights or even knife fights.

One evening, when it looked as though a fight was about to start, I decided (quite unwisely!) to wade in and try to stop it by exercising some clerical authority. One of the protagonists was most unimpressed by this and came at me swinging a punch. It was at this point that Christopher, our voluntary youth leader, interposed himself between me and my assailant, and in doing so collected a black eye. As I watched it develop during the next week, I could not help thinking, 'That's *my* black eye, but I haven't got it – Christopher has taken it for me.'

I have often used this story to get across something of the meaning of the cross. At its most basic level the cross is Jesus interposing himself between the human race and the trouble we have brought upon ourselves. He has collected much more than a black eye for you and me.

Young people can sometimes be more aware than others of the sin and folly that has brought so much suffering into the world. The Bible says that nobody is exempt: 'all have sinned and fall short of the glory of God' (Rom 3:23). That sin and folly should be the end of us, corporately and individually: 'the wages of sin is death' (6:23). Death of our spirit and extinction of our species is the logical, self-inflicted penalty of our rebellion against God and our flouting of his laws. Yet the miracle at the heart of the Christian faith is that Jesus has interposed himself between death and us: 'For God so loved the world that he gave his one and only Son, that whoever believes in him shall not perish but have eternal life' (John 3:16).

As a young person it is possible to make an act of personal assent to the one who lived and died and rose again to be our personal Saviour. What an investment this is! It is a great thing to move from youth into adulthood in the conviction that, whatever lies ahead, Jesus will be there with us as our companion on the way, as our guide and protector, as our Saviour in this world and the next. So spare a prayer for those who make it their life's work to communicate Christ to young people. It is a high calling and a difficult one.

Before ending this chapter I have three quotations to

share. Two are for those of us who are no longer teenagers. They may possibly serve to keep us just a little more humble, a little less judgemental.

> Past experience should be a guide post, not a
> hitching post.
>
> *D W Williams*

> Birthdays tell us how long we have been on the road,
> not how far we have travelled!
>
> *F W Boreham*

The other is from *The Lady's not for Burning* by Christopher Fry, and I offer it as a kind of parable. Two characters, Alizon and Thomas, are discussing the problems of life. Alizon is trying to persuade Thomas that life is worth living, but Thomas is feeling distinctly jaundiced. He says –

> 'Do you see those roofs and spires?
> There sleep hypocrisy, porcous pomposity, greed,
> Lust, vulgarity, cruelty, trickery, sham
> And all possible nitwittery – are you suggesting fifty
> Years of that?'

Alizon replies –

> 'No, I'm suggesting fifty years of me.'

To the teenager who feels like Thomas – who turns to Jesus in disillusionment asking, 'Are you suggesting fifty years of that?' – Jesus gives the same reply as Alizon: 'No, I'm suggesting fifty years of *me*.'

Chapter 3

DISCOVERING THE ADULT WORLD

If we are fortunate enough to discover Jesus in our youth, one of the gifts we may well bring to him is that of enthusiasm. I'm all for it. In fact, though a long way from being a teenager now, I am a thoroughgoing enthusiast for Christ myself – perhaps more than ever. So when I see young people whose emotions surge and whose eyes shine for Christ, I am thrilled. But enthusiasm on its own is not enough. It has to be backed up by perseverence. Jesus says, '...he who stands firm to the end will be saved' (Matt 10:22). Committed Christianity will always echo the prayer of Sir Francis Drake when he sailed into Cadiz in 1587:

> Lord God, when you give to your servants to
> endeavour any great matter, grant us also to know
> that it is not the beginning, but the continuing of the
> same, until it is thoroughly finished, which yields the
> true glory.

Some years ago, there was a vivacious group of young

people in the church where I was vicar. They used to
devise and present lively services for us, and travelled
around other churches, speaking about their faith. Older
Christians were sometimes reduced to tears by the sim-
plicity and enthusiasm of their words.

But those heady days came to an end. The glow faded.
The group broke up. We tried hard to keep in contact with
the members, but many of them went on to find other interests, other enthusiasms. Sadly, it *is* possible for love for the
Lord to grow cold (Matt 24:12).

As we move from our teenage years into adult life, it is
vital that our enthusiasm be fortified and refined by an
awareness of life's changing nature and God's developing
call; by a willingness to go on listening, learning and obey-
ing; by sheer, gritty stickability. And this is done not so
much by consciously holding onto our feelings of enthusiasm, as by holding onto Christ and letting him hold onto us.
'Christ with us' is the key. It is the practice of his presence
that brings us Christian perspective, direction and challenge
as we make the transition to the adult world.

I remember my own twenty-first birthday party and the
dewy-eyed expectations of life I had at that stage. I was to
learn all too soon that a whole new set of pressures lay wait-
ing round the corner. Paul urges the Christians of the first
century, 'Don't let the world around you squeeze you into
its own mould' (Rom 12:2, *J B Phillips*). This is a good
motto for us in our own day too, particularly for those who
are just beginning to explore adult life.

So in this chapter let's look at the relevance of these
words to two basic areas of life and experience – honesty
and sexuality. As we do so we can keep an eye on ourselves,
whatever our age, and see whether or not we have made
Paul's motto our own.

First, how do you and I score in the world of personal

honesty or dishonesty? Two very different men, whom I met in past years, come to mind. When I was a boy, one of them stole a shilling from me – twelve old pence, which was big money in those days. I put my shilling down on the counter of a shop because I wanted to buy some sweets, and he picked it up and pretended it was his own. I protested loudly, and was thrown out of the shop for my pains.

The other was a Cambridge watch-repairer I met when I was at theological college. My watch had stopped, so I took it to him and picked it up the next day in perfect working order. He charged me just six old pence. When I queried this, he said, 'It was a very small job. It was only worth six pence.' I pointed out that I would never have known. He answered, 'Well, *I* know it, and I'm the one who's got to live with myself!'

What a contrast! It seems that the honesty/dishonesty spectrum in our nation is a very wide one. It has been estimated that about one-third of the population consists of people who are basically honest. If they find a wallet containing banknotes in the park, they will hand it in at the police station or make some other effort to return it to its owner.

By contrast, another third of the population consists of people who are actively dishonest, who believe that honesty is a mug's game. They range from criminals who may end up in prison, to folk who would be regarded as ordinary citizens but who still put a great deal of thought and ingenuity into acquiring things that don't belong to them. Sometimes they don't think they are doing anything wrong. I remember an occasion when, during the course of visiting in one of my former parishes, I came across a house with impressive wooden panelling and furnishings. The man of the house told me with some pride that he had made it all himself and it had not cost him a penny because he had 'lifted' all the wood from the builder's yard where he worked. He was quite surprised when I didn't exactly enthuse about it!

The remaining third, while not actively dishonest, won't turn down a chance to be dishonest if it is presented to them on a plate. If they come across a wallet in the park, they will probably pocket any money it may contain. A recent *World in Action* programme investigating standards of honesty has suggested that this section of society numbers far more than one-third of the population and probably represents the norm in Britain today.

The eighth commandment is 'You shall not steal'. It was given by God to Moses (Exod 20:15), affirmed by Jesus (Mark 10:19), and hammered home by Paul (Rom 13:9; Eph 4:28). But if two-thirds or more of our population are either actively or passively dishonest, then as a nation we break God's law.

I would guess that you and I would hope to come into the actively honest section of the population. After all, I am writing this book about Christian living and you have been concerned enough to buy it and read it. But I wonder if, in spite of this, the world does sometimes manage to squeeze us into its mould. The *World in Action* programme reckoned that among the hundreds caught out in acts of petty dishonesty were several vicars! So let's check.

What about *petty* theft? If you are given too much change in a shop, do you automatically hand it back? If a letter arrives with an unfranked stamp on it, are you tempted to use it again?

What about *conventional* theft? It is so easily justified on the grounds that 'everybody does it'. Do you bring back 'perks' from work that are not really yours? How do you feel about the fact that the items on your income tax return are known *in detail* to God?

What about *collusive* theft? Do you find yourself saying

nothing about a dishonest industrial practice at work because if you do it might get you into trouble with management or the trade union?

What about the theft of *time?* The case of the employee who does less than the hours he is paid for, or the person who is always late for appointments and thus steals time from others?

What about the theft of *health*? The employer who disregards safety regulations, or the smoker who inflicts passive smoking on others?

What about the theft of *reputation*? Indulging in gossip? Christians are by no means immune to this failing. We say, 'I don't suppose there is anything in it, but I've heard...' or 'Of course I'm telling you this just for your prayers!'

What about the theft of *credit* that belongs to another? I once devised some discussion courses only to see them published with another Christian's name on them.

What about *stealing from God*? My guess is that the *majority* of Christians withhold money, time and talents from God which are his due. The prophet Malachi calls this theft (read Malachi 3:8–9 if you dare!).

So, what if you and I have caught ourselves out in being not quite as honest as we thought we were and are feeling a bit ashamed, a touch grubby? There is a simple gospel procedure you may find helpful, which consists of confessing our sins, asking for forgiveness in the name of Jesus, receiving forgiveness from the God who likes to say 'Yes', then getting on with life and having a go at doing better.

We can do this in the knowledge that honesty is *not* a mug's game. The mug's game is dishonesty. Industrial dishonesty puts prices up and quality down. Political dishonesty diminishes the whole nation. Criminal dishonesty damages innocent people and costs a fortune in court cases that must be paid for out of taxation. Dishonesty in shops and supermarkets involves a percentage rise in prices to off-set shoplifting and to pay for store detectives. Dishonesty in the home is a prime factor in the break-up of family life. As always, our Father knows best. Honesty really *is* the best policy.

My second illustration of an area of life in which the world tries to squeeze us into its mould is that of personal sexuality. Today's world approves and practises a policy of sexual permissiveness. We are brainwashed into it daily by the media. In television dramas and soap operas it is now commonplace for extramarital sex to be portrayed, some-times in a quite explicit fashion and often without any par-ticular relevance to the plot. The same is true of films and novels. In comedy shows, sniggering at sex often takes the place of real humour.

Sexual permissiveness is even infiltrating the Christian church. A fortnight before I wrote this chapter, the *Church Times* published an article in which a curate argued that these days it is unrealistic to tell young people to avoid sex-ual intercourse before marriage. He reports without regret that his own girlfriend was pregnant before they married, and makes the comment: 'The ideal of sexual union coin-ciding with legal marriage is romantic and morally tidy, but highly impractical and unlikely' (Paul Holley, *Church Times*, 14 February 1997).

In a climate such as this let me nail my own colours to the mast. What I am going to write is based on my total acceptance of the traditional Christian teaching that sexual-ity is God's good gift to us and sexual intercourse should take place only within marriage. I realise many will regard this as a simplistic and outdated statement. What is my basis for making it?

First, it is *biblical*. The Bible makes it clear that disci-plined sexual morality is a basic and necessary ingredient in any healthy society and that we abandon it at our peril both as individuals and as a nation. Paul's incisive instruction is 'Avoid sexual looseness like the plague!' (1 Cor 6:18, *J B Phillips*). Avoid practising it. Avoid talking about it. Avoid slavering over it.

> Live your lives in love – the same sort of love which Christ gave us … But as for sexual immorality in all its forms … don't even talk about such things…
> For of this you can be quite certain: that neither the immoral nor the dirty-minded nor the covetous man … has any inheritance in the kingdom of Christ and of God. Don't let anyone fool you with empty words.
>
> *Ephesians 5:2–6, J B Phillips*

Second, I believe in love, that 'God is love' and life is for loving (1 John 4:16; Mark 12:29–31). Sexual permissiveness, though it is sometimes called 'free love', is not a loving way of life. It is not loving to spread disease in the way that happens when the norm is to have a plurality of sexually active relationships. It is not loving to bring unwanted children into the world. (One in five conceptions now ends in abortion in England and Wales!) It is not loving to treat another human being as little more than a source of one's own gratification. Contraception does not provide an answer: contraceptives are not infallible and human beings are certainly not infallible in the use of them.

Third, many years of pastoral experience have led me to the conclusion that sexual permissiveness does not lead to happiness. 'Free love' does not lead to freedom. I think of Colin, scared to death because he thought he had a sexually transmitted disease. Or Judy, terrified she was pregnant and in a panic when her fear made her miss a couple of periods.

Or John and Sally who regularly had intercourse before they were married but found that after marriage they were incapable of it. They had preconditioned themselves to all the wrong surroundings and stimuli. They are divorced now. Emotional damage, physical damage and sociological damage follow sexual permissiveness as night follows day.

Fourth, and most significant in terms of the theme of this book, if I were to tell the Christ who is with me that I had decided to change my way of life to one of sexual permissiveness, I hardly think he would be happy about it. Jesus said, 'A man will leave his father and mother and be united to his wife, and the two will become one flesh. So they are no longer two, but one. Therefore what God has joined together, let man not separate' (Mark 10:7–9). Our sexuality is meant to lead to the closest relationship this world can hold, a relationship in which two people virtually become one. To squander it on anything less is to cheat ourselves. Next to the love of the Lord, the love of my wife Eira is the most precious thing in my life. I can never be sufficiently grateful to him for bringing us together. To exchange all we have together for the poisoned perks of permissive living would not only be disobedience to Christ, it would also be the poorest deal I could possibly imagine.

Before leaving this subject, let's look at three possible objections to traditional Christian sexual morality. Rod and Barbara come to mind. They sat in my study and said, 'We're in love. We're engaged. One day we'll be married. Going the whole way now can't possibly be wrong for us.' But are they right, even judged from the standpoint of their own satisfaction and fulfilment?

The thing about an engagement is that it is *not* the same as marriage. An engagement can be broken. Sometimes it should be broken. It is part of the concept of engagement that one can 'disengage' without spoiling another life or lessening the freshness and uniqueness of one's own marriage when it happens. The amount of joy we receive from sexual intercourse depends on the *meaning* it has for us. When it means complete self-giving, complete sharing, complete loving, complete commitment, it is a tremendous thing. Where commitment is incomplete, as it is in an engagement, intercourse has less meaning and is a lesser thing. Where commitment is nil, as in promiscuous sex, the sex act means little or nothing, and to throw away one's first experience of intercourse in this way is one of the saddest forms of waste.[1]

The second objection may come from the unmarried. A single man once said to me, 'It's all right for you – you're married, I'm not. When you talk to me about sex, it's like someone who regularly sits down to a steak dinner telling somebody else to be vegetarian!'

I have to admit the force of this comment. Maybe a book by a married man is not the place to make observations about the single life. However, there are one or two thoughts which may be useful and which I can make precisely because I am married.

We must not fall into the trap of somehow identifying our sense of being with our degree of sexual activity. Was Francis of Assisi less of a human being because he was not sexually active? Was Florence Nightingale? Or Mother Teresa? Or, for that matter, Jesus himself? Human nature is a many-splendoured thing, amazingly rich in potential. None of us will achieve our full potential in this life. To marry actually restricts our development in some ways. Because I am married to my wife, I have no right to be 'married to my work' or 'wedded to culture' or passionately attached to some hobby that takes me away from home at all hours. The single person is free to do these things, and I have met married people who have been distinctly envious of their single friends for just that reason.

The commitment of those who are married is a privilege. But the freedom of those who are single is also a privilege. It is the freedom to spend more time with friends, to develop and enjoy a special closeness of friendship which is denied to those who are married. It is the freedom to give priority to non-domestic concerns. It is the freedom to explore both the internal and the external world. It is the freedom to use money in a way that the married could not contemplate. It is the freedom not to get up in the middle of the night to change nappies. It is the freedom to go out when you want to and to stay in when you want to. It is the freedom to spend many hours in mental and spiritual development. It is the freedom to build up a unique relationship with the Christ who is with us: 'An unmarried man is concerned about the Lord's affairs – how he can please the Lord. But a married man is concerned about the affairs of this world – how he can please his wife' (1 Cor 7:32–33).

Don't get me wrong. I am thrilled with the joy that marital commitment has brought me, but not for a moment do I believe that there cannot be joy in any other context. And as for those who want to have their cake and eat it, to engage in full sexual activity but to make no commitment, I believe for all the reasons already stated that this is a recipe for disaster.

The third objection to traditional Christian morality is the widespread notion that chastity is just plain boring. All too often this objection is made without any thought whatsoever, but it still wields considerable power. I would not like to guess the number of people who have lost their sexual innocence simply because they did not want to be thought boring and conventional. But for any who may be experiencing this pressure here and now I believe I have good news. One of the few positive aspects about the downward moral path of today's society is that it is no longer conventional to be chaste. It is now rather excitingly original! The tired conventional pattern within society is now that of permissive sexuality. Those who stand out against it are much more likely to intrigue than to bore. Society's reaction may well be encapsulated in these words: 'Your innocence is on at such a rakish angle, It gives you quite an air of iniquity!' (Fry, *The Lady's not for Burning*).

I had wondered whether to call this chapter 'Decisions! Decisions!' because never at any other time in life are so many crucial choices demanded of us. Sexuality and honesty are just two areas in which choices have to be made as we enter adulthood. Other decisions are not primarily matters of ethics and morality: they are about the choices that determine how we will spend the rest of our lives. They are frighteningly important because we will suffer or benefit from them for years to come.

The good news is that we do not have to make these life-shaping decisions on our own. We may not ourselves have the wisdom and perspective we need, but if we are Christians we know someone who does! So, to end this chapter, let's construct a hypothetical situation to help us see the difference the presence of Jesus can make to the decision-making process.

You are in your mid-twenties. You have left your parents' home but live not far from them in your own flat. You have a job with which you are reasonably content. You have a circle of friends, including one who is becoming increasingly special to you – though neither of you has declared your feelings. Life is jogging along steadily enough. But then comes a total surprise, a bolt from the blue – the opportunity for a new job and a new life overseas. You have to make a decision. It will either cut you off from everything that is familiar, and radically change your life. Or, if you decide to turn the opportunity down, it may leave you wondering what you have missed for the rest of your days. So what are you going to choose and how are you going to do it?

May I suggest a process you may find useful? Take a large sheet of paper and divide it into two sections. At the top of one half write 'Pros', and at the top of the other write 'Cons'. Under 'Pros' list all the advantages you can think of, and under 'Cons' list all the disadvantages. Then lay it before the Lord and wait.

King Hezekiah does something of the sort in the Old Testament (2 Kings 18–19). His kingdom is under attack and Jerusalem, his capital city, is under siege. All around are the massive forces of the king of Assyria, forces that have already stormed and crushed city after city. The prospects are bleak and Hezekiah knows it. To make matters worse he has received a sneering, menacing letter from the Assyrians demanding unconditional surrender. Morale in the city is low. Hezekiah tears his clothes in despair. But then he pulls himself together, he goes to the temple, opens out the letter and 'spread[s] it out before the Lord'. He prays and he waits. And the situation becomes clearer and is changed in an amazing way.

We are more fortunate than Hezekiah. He could only spread out his letter before the shadowy God of the Old Testament. We can spread ours before our friend and companion-on-the-way, Jesus. In his presence we can open our Bibles and ask him to show us the scriptural truths he would want us to recognise and apply – as we do we will find our minds become clearer and our options plainer. As our minds are joined to the mind of Christ, we will find that his own distinctive input begins to become part of our thinking. When all the ingredients of the situation have marinated in his presence, we will find ourselves able to make our decision. If we stay, it will be because we believe we are where we are meant to be. If we go, we shall know that as we arrive Christ will be there ahead of us. As we practise his presence and walk in his way, it may not always be easy. But two things are promised. We will find that not only do we discover a life of real significance, we also grow closer to him:

> He comes to us as One unknown, without a name, as of old He came to those who knew him not … He speaks to us the same word, 'Follow me,' and sets us the tasks which He has to fulfil for our time. He commands. And to those who obey Him, whether they be wise or simple, He will reveal Himself in the toils, the conflicts, the sufferings which they shall pass through in His fellowship, and as an ineffable mystery, they shall learn in their own experience Who He is.
>
> *Albert Schweitzer*

Note

1 Those who have slept with someone before marriage and who repent of it can find forgiveness just as for any other repented sin. There is a prayer for forgiveness at the end of chapter nine which can be used at this point if it is appropriate. I have included chapters on forgiveness in my books, *How to Pray When Life Hurts* and *Make me a Channel*, Scripture Union, 1995, 1996.

Chapter 4

THE PRIME OF LIFE

You may possibly be feeling a touch uncomfortable after reading the last chapter. If so, then it is time for me to make a confession.

Before my ordination, Bishop George Sinker, who was back in England after serving in India as Bishop of Nagpur, came to conduct a retreat at my theological college. He took as his theme 'Practising the presence of Jesus', and during the time he spent with us he provided a list of practical methods by which each one of us could make this theme a personal reality. For example, he suggested that we might cultivate the practice, every time we opened a door, of saying the silent prayer: 'Jesus, come with me through this doorway'. We could harness the power of habit in this and other ways so as to ensure that we were conscious of Christ with us at every moment of every day and night.

It was during this retreat that I made a disturbing discovery about myself. It happened to me right in the middle of one of the bishop's addresses. Even though I was a full-time theological student and only months away from ordination to the ministry, I realised with some degree of horror that in fact I did not want to practise the presence of Jesus at every moment of every day and every night. There were parts of my life I wanted to keep to myself.

I have always believed in trying to be honest with God, so during my next time of private prayer I brought this unwelcome revelation to him to see what he would say about it. And it seemed to me that what he said was this.

'It's all right, Roy – for now, at any rate. None of what you have said is unknown to me, and I am pleased that you have come to know it too. I have always been ready to accept those things you have brought to me with pleasure, even though it has been a partial offering.

'You are like a rambling house in which I have been invited through the front door and into some of the rooms. I stand at each door and knock. But I will never force my way into any of those rooms. I will never be an uninvited guest. You are, and will always be, free.

'But know this – if the house is to be mine, sooner or later all the doors must open. Ultimately, in time or in eternity, I must have all of you – or none of you.'

As these words entered my mind, they reminded me that Jesus wants to be not just beside me, but *in*side me, releasing me from all that binds me, filling every part of me with his light and his life. Since then my life has involved gradually opening one door after another to Jesus. I have often been tardy in doing so. I have sometimes been extremely ungracious. But I can honestly say that I have never regretted opening a door to him, whereas I have often regretted not opening one sooner than I did.

I wonder whether God could be saying something similar to you at this time. This door-opening process is a basic ingredient of Christian living and perhaps especially so in our thirties and forties, those years that are sometimes regarded as the prime of life. These are meant to be the years of growing Christian maturity. As one thinks about them, key words come to mind. 'Responsibility' is one, and it is a different sort of responsibility from that we may have encountered in our twenties. Then, as we discovered adult life, we had to learn to be responsible for ourselves. But as we move into our thirties and forties, increasingly we find ourselves responsible for others too.

As this happens we may encounter new kinds of worry – worry about our family, our friends, our work, our competence to cope with the responsibilities we have for those who depend on us. Against this background the biblical challenge is to 'become mature, attaining to the whole measure of the fulness of Christ' (Eph 4:13). Of course, this would be impossible in our own strength. But the experience of 'Christ with us' can make a transforming difference as we tackle these new responsibilities and worries.

By the time I reached my early thirties, I was married to Eira and we had two little boys. Our first, Christopher, was a strapping healthy lad, but our second son, Paul, had to face a life-threatening illness. For six months we would put him to bed at night and not know for certain whether he would be alive in the morning.

In all honesty we could not say, 'Why should this happen to us?' By then I was vicar of my first parish, a parish in which there were many, many children. We had seen similar things happen to others who did not deserve it. We knew there was no reason why we should be exempt. Also, by reason of my job, I had been forced to think hard about this sort of situation well in advance. I had had to write essays about it at theological college! I knew at a mental level that if God were to make a world in which freedom was a real factor, then that world must have a built-in element of risk. In a free world all kinds of things can go wrong, all kinds of suffering can take place. Only free people can learn to love and be loved. So the risk involved in this terrible gift of freedom is worthwhile.

Of course, dealing with a situation in theory is one thing. Coping with it in practice is another. It is not easy to think and react in a straightforward fashion when you feel sad and helpless and uncertain and tired and scared. Various things helped us to cope.

It helped to have something to do – and there is always plenty to do on occasions of stress and illness, if we keep our eyes open. There is the provision of proper medical attention and personal care for the one who is ill, and life must go on for the rest of the family too. Doing something useful is no more exhausting than wringing one's hands, and a good deal more practical. Also, oddly enough, we found it helped to face the possibility of the worst. One of the things that can make us tired and ill at a time of family crisis is the bottling up and holding in of our fears. They are much better out in the open. Once we have faced the worst, any little progress is a tonic.

We found it helpful to live one day at a time. There was a lot of sense in the words of Cardinal Newman's famous hymn: 'I do not ask to see the distant scene; one step enough for me'.

However, what helped us most to look at the situation squarely was the feeling that we were able to share it with God through the Christ who was with us. We felt we could go to God not only because we believed him to be strong and loving, but because he watched his own Son suffer. He understood what we were going through. Where we could neither help nor cope, we left the situation with God in prayer. We asked others to pray too, and we learned to rest in the knowledge that they were doing so. The Scargill community prayed for us, as did a group of Franciscans. And our little boy got better. In time he became as scruffy and energetic as his brother. Ultimately, they both grew up and got married.

So this particular story has a happy ending, though we could have no certainty that it would do so at the time. In this life you never know what lies around the corner. But Jesus knows. And as we approach the next corner in life, the one assurance we can have as Christians is that we shall find him there, the Christ who is with us.

Life in his presence can involve a strange mixture. During our years in ministry, Eira and I have encountered two very different sorts of experience. For there are two contrasting truths about Christian living. This is perhaps the right place to deal with them both.

First, let it be stressed that it is a wonderful thing to have Jesus at the heart of life. We could have no lovelier or livelier companion on the way. We must beware of being taken in by pallid, negative images of Jesus, like that in the famous line of verse by the poet Algernon Charles Swinburne: 'Thou hast conquered, O pale Galilean; the world has grown grey from thy breath...' Lord Hailsham has offered an exuberant corrective to this in his autobiographical book, *The Door Wherein I Went*:

Jesus was irresistibly attractive as a man ... full of life and the joy of it, the Lord of life itself, and even more the Lord of laughter, someone so utterly attractive that people followed him for the sheer fun of it ... the twentieth century needs to recapture the vision of this glorious and happy man, whose presence filled his companions with delight. No pale Galilean he, but a veritable Pied Piper of Hamelin, who would have the children laughing all round him and squealing with pleasure and joy as he picked them up.

The company of such a man has to be the most positive of all experiences. In the words of Pope John XXIII: 'Christianity ... is peace, joy, love and a life which is continually renewed, like the mysterious pulse of nature at the beginning of spring'. What more could we want for our prime of life than the knowledge of such a Christ with us? Eira and I have benefited so much from the gifts that have come to us in his presence. Again and again we have had reason to be grateful for what he has done for us at a spiritual, physical, mental and even financial level. And apart from all we have received from him, it has been so good just to have him around.

Many others have found this to be so in their own experience. Bernard, who was churchwarden in a parish where I used to work, was a very successful and respected businessman. One day when I was visiting him, I asked him what he thought was the reason for his success. He answered, 'I suppose it is because people feel they can trust me.' Then after a pause he added, 'And, you know, I owe that trustworthiness entirely to Jesus.' Bernard clearly understood what Dick Sheppard meant when he wrote, 'The world will be at the feet of those who are themselves at the feet of Jesus – that is the surest thing I know'.

Many books have been written about the blessings that come to those who put their trust in Jesus, and one of the most famous is Norman Vincent Peale's *The Power of Positive Thinking*. Dr Peale believes that the Christian faith provides the prescription for upbeat, effective living. The blurb on the cover promises readers ten rules for developing confidence, three secrets for keeping up your vigour, four words that lead to success, five techniques to overcome defeat, and much more besides.

I am sure it is all true, but it is only half the truth. Jesus certainly tells us his aim – 'that my joy may be in you and that your joy may be complete' (John 15:11). But he also says, 'In this world you will have trouble' (John 16:33). So let me now add the stories of two other churchwardens, to provide something of a contrast to Bernard. Both these men found themselves facing considerable trouble for Jesus' sake.

I met Stanley before I was ordained. He was churchwarden at a mission church where I was occasionally invited to assist at services. I came to have considerable respect for Stanley. He resigned from the firm he worked for on a point of principle, because he believed the company to be guilty of serious malpractice. He knew he was taking a risk – there was a chance his name would be blackened and it would be hard for him to find other work. But he felt as a Christian he had to make a stand.

To be without a job and a reference was not easy, but worse was to come. Soon after his resignation he became ill. The cause was difficult to trace, but he was told by his doctor that it might be some sort of viral infection. Stanley became housebound. Pains in his back and limbs kept him in continuous discomfort. The condition did not respond to treatment. For month after month there was no improvement. His wife became increasingly worried. The family finances were draining away. Stanley's own spirit sank lower and lower.

Then one day, when I was visiting him, he said to me, 'You know, if Jesus was here, he'd shift all this. He'd heal me.' We thought about this in silence for a while, and then it struck us both together. We both believed in the Christian doctrine of 'Christ with us'.

Jesus was there. We had his word for it: 'where two or three come together in my name, there am I with them' (Matt 18:20). And we two were together in his name. We soon knew what we had to do.

The next day we both spent the morning in prayer, I in the parish church and Stanley at home. In the afternoon I laid hands on him in the name of the Christ who was with us. He started to improve almost immediately. A fortnight later he was riding his bicycle around the parish! Soon afterwards he and his wife and little boy went on a celebratory holiday. While they were away, he was offered a better job than his old one by someone who just happened to be on holiday at the same hotel and who got to know him.

So Stanley's story had a happy ending, but not before he had faced months of stress, conflict and illness for the sake of Christ.

Stanley found that his Christian convictions brought him into conflict with management, but in Doug's case the conflict was with his trade union. Everybody was delighted when Doug agreed to be our churchwarden because he was an easygoing and popular man. He was well liked in the local factory where he worked and would not have been regarded as a troublemaker by anyone. When his trade union called a strike, he was not happy about it but he came out to show solidarity with the rest. It was when the strike came to an end that he found himself in trouble.

The lady who made the tea in the canteen had continued to go in and brew up for the management while the strike was going on. When it was called off, the union decided she must be punished. The other workers were instructed to cut her dead. They were not to speak to her, and if she tried to speak to them they were to refuse to answer. She was to be treated as an outcast, an enemy.

One day Doug found her in tears in the corner of the canteen. He had not agreed with the course she took during the strike, but he felt she had been punished enough. He believed the only Christian thing to do was to offer her a few words of comfort, to tell her he was sure the punishment would not go on for ever. He was seen doing so by a union official and the upshot was that the instruction went out that nobody should speak to Doug either. He too was to be treated as an enemy, even though he had stood shoulder to shoulder with the others during the strike.

Doug was devastated and, like Stanley, he became ill. His doctor called the condition *ankylosing spondylitis* and prescribed a surgical collar. However, he told Doug that he wasn't sure a cure was possible. It all became too much for Doug and, like Stanley, he felt he had to hand in his notice.

When I went round to see him, depressed, jobless and in pain, it seemed right to tell him Stanley's story. Once again we agreed that we would pray, practising the presence of Jesus as we did so. Then I would lay hands on him for his healing. It is good to be able to report that the condition was swiftly healed. Soon afterwards Doug and his wife found a little corner shop for sale; they bought it and ran it successfully together.

We should not be surprised when the ministry of Christian healing makes a difference in circumstances such as those encountered by Stanley and Doug. If we believe that Jesus regularly healed the sick, that he is truly present when two or three come together in his name, that he has not changed but 'is the same yesterday and today and for ever' (Heb 13:8), then his healing influence should not be an uncommon Christian experience. I am convinced that the recovery of a sensible, scriptural healing ministry is a major call of God to the church today.[1]

However, we cannot take it for granted that all stories of Christians undergoing trouble will have happy endings. Some of the greatest Christians have been called to a special sort of identification with the sufferings of Jesus who said, 'If anyone would come after me, he must deny himself and take up his cross and follow me' (Matt 16:24). Paul calls it filling up 'what is still lacking in regard to Christ's afflictions' (Col 1:24). It is a great and dark mystery of which Martin Luther King knew something. In his book *Strength to Love* he wrote, 'I have known very few quiet days in the last few years. I have been imprisoned in Alabama and Georgia jails twelve times. My home has been bombed twice. A day seldom passes that my family and I are not recipients of threats of death. I have been the victim of a near-fatal stabbing.' As we know, he was assassinated on 4 April 1968 in Memphis, Tennessee.

Even in my own low-grade Christian experience there have been moments of almost intolerable anguish for the sake of Jesus, days when I did not know where to turn, nights when Eira has sobbed herself to sleep. This too can be part of knowing a growing union with the Christ who is with us, and it would be dishonest if I were to write about the joy of being one with him without also speaking of the cost. Yet those who share something of the cross of Jesus are often strangely aware of a sense of privilege in doing so. Paul actually says he rejoices in it (Col 1:24). How can this be? Listen to the words of that underrated writer, Dorothy L Sayers, in *The Zeal of Thy House*:

> Be comforted, thou that wast rich in gifts;
> For thou art broken on the self-same rack
> That broke the richest Prince of all the world,
> The Master-man. Thou shalt not surely die,
> Save as He died: nor suffer, save with Him;
> Nor lie in hell, for He hath conquered hell
> And flung the gates wide open. They that bear
> The cross with Him, with Him shall wear a crown
> Such as angels know not. Then be still,
> And know that He is God, and God alone.

Jesus put it all in perspective for his disciples when he spoke to them just before his death: 'I have told you these things, so that in me you may have peace. In this world you will have trouble. But take heart! I have overcome the world' (John 16:33).

So where does this leave us, ordinary folk like me and you?

I hope it leaves us praying for all who are called to share Christ's suffering. In our day and age more do so than we may realise. There have been more Christian martyrs in the twentieth century than in any other since Jesus' life and death. Less than a month before I wrote this chapter, twelve Egyptian Coptic Christians were gunned down by Islamic extremists while they were attending church. It was good to hear that almost immediately joint Christian and Muslim groups in Bradford and Manchester denounced violence of this sort. So many of us seem to give so little time and thought and prayer to the persecution that many of our brothers and sisters are experiencing in the name of Christ.

If it should be that we ourselves are bearing some sort of discomfort for Jesus' sake, then I hope this chapter will be an encouragement. We are not alone. It has never been an easy thing to journey with Jesus. The walk can sometimes slow to a limp while the world dashes by. But, in the words of John Calvin, 'It is better to limp along the path of God's way than to dash with all speed outside it'.

Finally, if it should be that we have never borne any sort of discomfort with or for Jesus, maybe this chapter is meant to bring us a personal challenge. There is a saying: 'No pain, no gain'. Those who made a stand for racial equality in South Africa during the days of apartheid would have agreed, as would those who stood for freedom in Beijing's Tiananmen Square. But what about you and me? What level of risk are we prepared to accept for Jesus' sake? As

Christian warriors, have we any scars of honour? Are we warriors at all – or just wimps?

Note

1 I have written in detail about this conviction in *The Practice of Christian Healing*, Inter-Varsity Press (US), 1996, available in the UK through Scripture Press.

Chapter 5

IS THIS IT?

I had just celebrated my fiftieth birthday, and I will never forget two calls I made during the days that followed as I was visiting in my parish.

The first was to a large house in our most salubrious area, to see a business man who had a slight connection with the church. I estimated that he was in his late fifties and I joked about joining the Fifty Club myself. But he was not amused. When I told him my age, he pulled a face and said, 'That's bad news. There's not much left in life once you're past fifty.'

The other visit, by contrast, was to an older lady who had been widowed and lived on her own in a little flat. When I told her about my birthday she positively glowed and said, 'I remember being fifty. It's a lovely age. You enjoy it!'

Which response strikes a chord with you? My guess is that the majority of people would tend to identify with the business man. The fifties and early sixties are sometimes known as the 'plateau years': though a few people continue to climb the professional ladder, most of us have to face the fact that we have got as far as we are going to get. Earlier in life it may be possible to hope or imagine that we are on the way to the highest places within our chosen sphere in life. In our fifties and early sixties it dawns on us that we are not going to be field marshals, or archbishops, or cabinet ministers, or captains of industry, or international stars, or whatever our dream may have been. The way we are is the way we are likely to remain. We have reached 'the plateau'.

This may involve dealing with a real sense of disappointment and depression. We may ask ourselves, 'Is this it? Is this all there is to life?'

For married couples there may also be the adjustment to children leaving home. Husband and wife are left looking across the breakfast table at each other, seeing warts and all, and perhaps again asking, 'Is this it?'

Then there is the possibility of voluntary or not-so-voluntary redundancy rearing its head at work. Of course, it can happen at any age. Two of my friends, who are in the prime of life, are struggling with redundancy as I write, and are finding it highly traumatic. But the risk increases in the fifties and early sixties, when any industrial restructuring tends to favour those who are younger and more technologically advanced. When you add to all of this the fact that at this stage we are past our physical peak, sexual attractiveness is waning, mental agility may not be what it was, energy levels are declining, and society is changing bewilderingly, it is not surprising that for some people these years can be a time of real personal crisis. However, it is possible to turn the crisis into an opportunity for exciting and life-transforming discovery. It is at this period that we can learn the lesson that the secret of life lies more in *being* than in *doing*.

Mind you, many of us have problems with the challenge this presents. It is neatly summed up by John Powell SJ in his book *Why am I Afraid to Tell You Who I am?* His answer: 'I am afraid to tell you who I am, because if I tell you who I am, you may not like who I am, and it's all that I have'. In other words, we are likely to be reluctant to move from an emphasis on doing to an emphasis on being if we have a low sense of self-esteem – and the majority of people probably have just that.

For many years one of my pet hates was the moment at the start of conferences when the leader goes round the room and says to each participant, 'Tell the group who you are and say a little bit about yourself.' I always felt this was a great moment to go to the loo!

When I thought about it, I could see that the embarassment I felt was a symptom of low self-esteem on my part. It was difficult to deal with because it went back to some of my earliest experiences of life. Mercifully, God decided to take a hand in the situation, though I have to say that I did not much like it when he did. I was kneeling in church at the time, saying my morning prayers, when it seemed that he spoke to me. There was no audible voice or anything like that, just a question forming in my mind. I am not one who can normally claim to have a hot-line to God, but I was quite sure this question came from God and it initiated a sort of dialogue inside my head. I remember exactly how it went.

'Who are you?' asked God.

Fumblingly I answered, 'You know who I am, Lord. You have put me here. I'm the vicar of this parish.'

'No,' said God, 'I didn't ask *what* you are. *Who* are you?'

I blundered on: 'I'm Eira's husband. I'm father to Christopher and Paul.'

'And they are all precious to me,' said God. 'But for this moment I am not asking about them.

'Who are *you* ?'

As the conversation went on, gradually he stripped everything away from me – background, qualifications, achievements: 'Not *what*? *Who*?'

Finally I said, 'I'm Roy.'

There was silence. I felt so empty and insignificant. Then came his word again, 'Yes, you are Roy. Whom I created with infinite care, whom I love, and for whom I gave my Son, Jesus. And whom I call to be one with me in time and in eternity.'

That was it. The dialogue was over.

God may not always like me any more than I always like myself. But he loves me and values me, and I knew then that I had to learn to value myself too. To fail to do so would not be pious humility: it would be an impious claim to know better than God. It would be tantamount to blasphemy!

God made us. God loves us. God wants us. We are worthwhile people. Sinners, yes, but sinners worth saving, infinitely precious to God. This is the message of the Christ with us, who loves us and has laid down his life for us (John 15:9,13), who accepts us here and now just as we are (Rom 15:7). He will not rest until he has cleansed us and worked out his amazing purpose for us, the like of which we could not even begin to conceive with our present limited minds (1 John 1:9; 3:2).

So we do not have to cower away from self-knowledge. We do not have to hide behind a palisade of pretence. Neither do we have to retreat from reality into a world of mental fantasy, or anaesthetise ourselves against inner truth by frenetic workaholism.

Not that life with Jesus will ever be static or inactive. For myself, I think I was busier during my fifties and early sixties than at any other time. I was presiding over what the diocese called 'a major parish'. I was being invited far and wide, at home and abroad, to share some of the truths I had learned about the Christian healing ministry. I had been made an honorary canon of Chester Cathedral, and had diocesan as well as parish duties. Rightly or wrongly, I was invited to help train other, younger clergy. I met with dozens of curates from other parishes and, over the years, I had twenty-one curates of my own. I was privileged to develop a writing ministry. My personal record was the publication of three books in a single year and that happened in my last year as a parish vicar at the age of sixty-four. The hours I was working would have made any trade unionist blanch!

But, at the same time, God was inexorably hammering home to me the truth that at root *being* is more important than *doing*. We are all made in the image of God (Gen 1:27), and he calls us to recognise and recover that image by the saving power of Jesus. This is meant to be a fundamental item on the human agenda at every stage of life, but never more so than when we are in our fifties and early sixties. The principal challenge of these years lies in God's call to face inner reality. So what about you and me? Are we daring to be real people?

I invite you to run a reality check on yourself and on your faith. True religion makes us real people, whereas false religion panders to our neuroses, defence mechanisms and prejudices. False religion fortifies unreality. Nevertheless, we are sometimes tempted to prefer false religion, because reality can hurt. Margery Williams writes wisely and poignantly about becoming real in *The Velveteen Rabbit*. I leave her words to speak for themselves:[1]

'Does it hurt?' asked the Rabbit.
'Sometimes,' said the Skin Horse, for he was always truthful. 'When you are real, you don't mind being hurt.'

'Does it happen all at once, like being wound up,' he asked, 'or bit by bit?'

'It doesn't happen all at once,' said the Skin Horse. 'You become. It takes a long time. That's why it doesn't often happen to people who break easily, or have sharp edges, or have to be carefully kept. Generally, by the time you are Real, most of your hair has been loved off, and your eyes drop out and you get loose in the joints and very shabby. But these things don't matter, because once you are Real you can't be ugly, except to people who don't understand.'

Reality is worth any pain it may involve, because self-deception and prejudice ultimately enslave, whereas Jesus is the essence of truth (John 14:6) and the truth sets you free (John 8:32). Given half a chance, Jesus will always increase our freedom level. He will make us free to love, free to learn and free to laugh – especially at ourselves. There can be real joy in this. I love the words of John Powell in *The Christian Vision*: 'Blessed are they who can laugh at themselves, for they shall never cease to be entertained'.

Jesus will make us free to cut the things of this world down to size. Former archbishop Dr Donald Coggan has written: 'Man is becoming absorbed with things rather than with conviction; with the verb "to have" rather than the verb "to be"; with goods rather than with character and destiny. And that, of course, is the damnation of a man or a society.' Jesus offers to save us from that damnation.

Conversely, Jesus will make us free to take the things that are greater than this world more seriously – our spirituality, our sense of God's plan and perspective for our souls, our self-transcending awareness of those things that really matter in time and in eternity, our developing life of prayer.

I was in my fifties when I felt moved to conduct a two-year school of prayer. Once a month I met with members of my congregation and, instead of our normal Sunday evening service, we held 'workshops' in which a series of methods of prayer were explained and experienced. After notes had been distributed and instruction given, each participant would go to a different part of the church and try out the evening's prayer method. We would then come together to share our feelings and experiences in the hope that we could learn and grow together.

In view of the theme of this book, it will come as no surprise to learn that we discovered the essence of Christian prayer is the practice of the presence of Christ. As we practised his presence, we found that there were two ways forward. One was to contemplate a basic Christian truth such as the concept of the peace of God or the doctrine of the Holy Spirit. It became our experience that any Christian truth contemplated in the presence of Jesus yielded new treasures and assumed new relevance.

The other way forward was to bring our current state of life and experience into the presence of Jesus so that he could meet us at the point of our need. For instance, we looked at how to pray when you feel guilty and ashamed, how to pray when you feel angry or depressed, how to pray when you are anxious or fearful, how to pray when you are busy or stressed, how to pray when you feel jealous or envious, how to pray when you or others are ill, how to pray in bereavement. We found a considerable difference between life faced alone and life faced in the knowledge and experience of Christ with us. By the end of the school of prayer I had certainly moved forward spiritually. I hope that others had done so too.

Being human is never meant to be a static experience: we are meant to grow. Once, when I was away from home for a while, Eira sent me a card. On it were these words: 'Be patient with me. God hasn't finished with me yet'. Probably it would have been more fitting if I had sent it to her. But it's true of us all, and God seems to want to bring it to our attention particularly when we have passed life's mid-point.

Psychologists as well as theologians have noticed this. Carl Gustav Jung taught that without spiritual discovery and growth there can be no human fulfilment, and life becomes increasingly unsatisfactory for those who ignore the deeper needs of the soul. 'Among all my patients in the second half of life – that is to say over 35 – there has not been one,' he writes, 'whose problem in the last resort was not that of finding a religious outlook on life. It is safe to say that every one of them felt ill because he had lost that which the living religions of every age have given to their followers, and none of them has really been healed who did not regain their religious outlook.'

There is more to human life and human nature than meets the eye. We are more than skin-deep, you and I, and to explore what lies beneath the skin is one of life's most challenging enterprises. Courage is required in order to do this with total honesty, but it is the Christian's privilege to find that courage through the saving power of the Christ who is with us. It is his light that we are invited to shine upon the deep, dark places of our inner selves. It is his love that beckons us upwards and onwards. We are meant to become aware of this in a newer, deeper way as we move through our fifties and into our sixties. The lady I quoted at the beginning of this chapter was right. This can be a lovely time of life, an exciting time of life. So live it to the full. Don't undervalue it, but enjoy it!

Note

1 Margery Williams, *The Velveteen Rabbit*, William Heinemann Ltd, reproduced here by permission of Reed Books.

Chapter 6

RETIRING – OR ADVANCING?

I am pleased to have come to this chapter about the retirement years because this is the stage in life I am actually experiencing as I write this book. Three months ago I celebrated my sixty-fifth birthday and retired from full-time parish ministry. Up to a few years ago I would not have fancied the concept of retirement at all, but I have to tell you that so far I am relishing it in every way. Although I have given up the pressures of being a full-time vicar, I have not given up ministry and I have certainly not retired from life. In fact I have more time now for the things that matter, and can see that, paradoxically, retiring brings an opportunity for advancing.

One of the keynotes of life in retirement is freedom – the freedom for leisure, for family concerns, for time with friends, for becoming more truly human oneself and, above all, the freedom to ask the Christ who is with us, 'What shall you and I together do next?' This is a question never asked in vain.

However, having said this, I have to admit that whereas

so far I have been writing on the basis of long-term experience and measured thought, I am now in the world of short-term experience and day-to-day discovery. For that reason in this chapter I shall be augmenting my own conclusions, such as they are, with the wisdom of others who know far more about retirement than I do.

Many things, of course, have not changed. Jesus does not change, and the basic principles of Christian living do not change. Some of them seem to me to be particularly worth re-stating. For instance, retirement must be a good time to remember that Christians are always called to live in the present. It is neither healthy nor productive to live in the past, to continually hark back to the 'good old days', any more than it is healthy or productive to dwell on a hypothetical future, to miss out on today because of a preoccupation with what Lewis Carroll called 'jam tomorrow'.

In retirement, as always, it is vital to make the present count for something. 'Today' is an important biblical word. 'Today,' says the psalmist, 'if you hear his voice, do not harden your hearts'(Ps 95:7–8). The writer to the Hebrews places great stress on this verse, quoting it three times (Heb 3:7–8,15; 4:7); he urges his readers, 'Encourage one another daily, as long as it is called Today' (3:13). Paul comments, 'Now is the time of God's favour, now is the day of salvation' (2 Cor 6:2). The here and now is what we have got, you and I, at this precise moment in time. To waste the here and now is to waste life.

We waste the present if we look upon it with too jaundiced an eye, something humankind has always tended to do. If you are tempted to cry out, 'My God! What a century you have chosen for me to live in', it is good to remember that Polycarp used exactly those words in AD150!

So, whatever stage of life we may be in at present, how can we learn to maximise our time? For a start, we can learn from those who have done well with it, and this is where I call my first three witnesses. They are all people who have learned to maximise the retirement years.

Let me introduce you to my good friend, Trevor Griffiths, who has been retired for fourteen years. They have not been easy years for him. He has had to cope with a colostomy following a major operation, and he has had to look after a wife who increasingly suffers from dementia. Yet his retirement has been and still is a triumph. He has lived a full life and served the community in many ways, including several years as a vigorous and beloved church-warden in my last parish. Trevor radiates happiness and has a talent for helping others to be happy too.

Three months ago he sent me this prescription for a satisfying retirement:

1 Have a certain amount of daily routine to give one's day a shape.
2 Achieve at least one irksome task each day because it is good for morale when completed.
3 Make some positive attempt each day to give help or pleasure to others.
4 Provide a highlight for each day to ensure happy anticipation.
5 Keep body and mind as active as possible to enable the spirit to thrive.
6 Above all, have *complete faith* in *God's love*.

To me, as a beginner in the experience of retirement, it seems very sound advice. As far as point number 6 is concerned, it really is an asset to have extra, unpressured time to increase and refine one's personal faith, and to live in the presence of the *real* Jesus with whom we are journeying. It is worth dwelling on this thought for a while because its relevance is certainly not restricted to the retirement years.

How can we be sure that the Christ in our minds and hearts *is* the real Jesus? There are certainly many false notions about Christ and many false pictures of him. We have already rejected Swinburne's picture of the 'pale Galilean', the unreal, stained-glass-window figure whom you could never imagine sweating, laughing or living anything like an ordinary life. Here is no true incarnation but the product either of bogus pietism or, in the case of Swinburne, of pagan misrepresentation.

Or there is the idea – perhaps founded on a wrong interpretation of the hymn 'Gentle Jesus, meek and mild' – of Jesus the 'sissy', who wouldn't say boo to a goose. He could be gentle, of course, and we all have cause to be grateful for that. But he could also take a scourge and drive those who were commercialising and exploiting religion out of the temple (Mark 11:12–17).

There is the middle-class, respectable Christ who comforts and buttresses conventional prejudice. This kind of Jesus does not accord with scriptural record. The real Jesus made it plain that he had not come to call the respectable and righteous (Luke 5:32), and the leading citizens of the day made it plain that they wanted to be rid of him (19:47).

By contrast, there is the left-wing, 'Che Guevara', guerrilla-type Christ who would have had no sympathy with the respect the real Jesus showed for civic and religious authority, and who would have wasted no time loving his enemies.

There is the narrow-minded bigot who would never have gone to parties, who would have been keener to turn wine into water than vice versa. It is a startling thought that when Jesus' enemies wanted to throw insults at him, they called him 'a glutton and a drunkard' (Matt 11:19)!

There is the popular version of Jesus as a good, kind, home-spun philosopher whom nobody could possibly have wanted to crucify, a sentimental rather than scriptural figure.

So what sort of a person is Jesus? He defies type-casting. He is himself – unique, the Son of God and Son of Man, absolutely real in terms of the Godhead, absolutely real in terms of manhood, infinitely beyond us and yet miraculously available to us. The supreme privilege of Christian life and experience is to discover him and to know he has discovered us.

We discover the real Christ in a variety of ways.

We discover him as we read the Bible, the supreme source both of historical information about him, and of inspired reflection on that information. All Christians are called to be avid and grateful students of scripture, and the world ignores the Bible at its peril.

We discover Jesus in other Christian writings. In fact it is my hope and prayer that you may catch glimpses of him while you turn the fallible pages of this book.

We discover him in nature – after all, he had a major hand in its design (John 1:3) – and in great art, literature and music, works of creation that require a measure of contact with the Creator, consciously or unconsciously.

We discover him in the lives and personalities of every human being who has taken him seriously and responded to him positively. If we ourselves are Christians and believe in the truth of 'Christ with us', we discover him in our own times of prayer and reflection, and in our daily walk with God. The term 'walk with God' has a rather old-fashioned ring to it, but it is rich in meaning. I love the hymn by A H Ackley with its famous chorus:

He lives, He lives, Christ Jesus lives today.
He walks with me and talks with me along life's
   narrow way.

We are meant to walk with Jesus all through our life, coming to know the inner truth of him as we do so. Every stage brings its own opportunities, but I am pleased to find that retirement provides special facilities for this, sometimes in quite a literal fashion. Almost every day I can now spend an hour walking along the front near New Brighton, and as I walk I chat away to Jesus. It is, of course, an inner dialogue, or at any rate I try to keep it so, particularly if other people are around!

Wherever we are in life, we are all called to find our own way of Christian exploration, our own personal relationship with the Christ who is with us, our own steady growth in the knowledge of him and of his purpose for us. You might like to put this book down for a moment and challenge yourself with questions like 'What new truth have I learned about Jesus in the past week, or in the past month, or in the past year? How has my relationship with him deepened and developed? If there is no sign of new truth, new depth, new development, what should I be doing about it?'

But now, returning to the theme of retirement, it is time to bring on my second witness, Anne Mustoe. Anne and I met a few years before I retired, when she was invited to be the speaker at the prize-giving service at a local school where I acted as honorary chaplain.

You might expect that, as we consider the retirement years, this chapter will re-emphasise the point made in chapter five about the importance of *being* in contrast to *doing*. Certainly everything that was said there remains as true and significant in the later years as at any other stage in life. However, Anne represents a very different viewpoint on retirement. When she retired as headmistress of St Felix School in Southwold, she launched herself into a series of quite amazing adventures. The first, would you believe it, was a solo cycle-ride around the world! This was followed by a cycle-ride from Rome to Lisbon and another from the North to the South of India. She tells her story in her book, *A Bike Ride: 12,000 miles around the world* (Virgin, 1991).

At the speech day in our local school she challenged the school-leavers to be explorers during their student years. But, she added, if they missed that chance, a second window of opportunity would open for them at retirement! As she said goodbye to me after the service, she looked me in the eye and said, 'Your window of opportunity will be opening soon. Don't miss it!'

So who knows what may lie ahead?

Actually, I have already undertaken my own first act of exploration, and it hasn't even involved leaving home. For years and years I have been not only completely ignorant of the world of computers but also rather scared of it. As retirement came into sight, I decided something had to be done about this. First, I attended a basic computer course laid on by our local sixth-form college. Then I bought myself a computer, complete with an AmiPro wordprocessing programme, and a book entitled *The Complete Idiot's Guide to AmiPro*.

Thus equipped, I started my exploration and now, three months into retirement, I am able to announce that for the first time in my life I am actually computer-literate. The book you are reading is proof of this. The manuscript has been produced by me on my own computer, and very proud I am of it!

If you believe in the concept of 'Christ with us', no exploration is a solo affair. I believe that Jesus has sat with me in my study as I have explored my computer's inner world, and it has been quite a relief to have someone other than the computer to talk to! I am not called to be a lone explorer. If I am a Christian believing that Christ is with me, any adventure should be in his service and every exploration will be a journey at his side.

All of which brings me to my third witness, the late Dr Noel Fletcher who worked for many years in India for the Church Mission Society and then came back to this country to retire. Eira and I were once privileged to welcome Noel as our house guest when she was on home-leave from her missionary work. Later, when she came back to Britain to retire, she became a dear and close friend.

The main thing we learned from her was that a Christian need never fear the future. She had embodied this principle in the sometimes hazardous life she had led as a missionary doctor, and she continued to embody it when she retired. One day when we visited her in her flat in Stockport, she shared one of her favourite quotations with us. 'One day you may need this,' she said, and she put into my hands a little piece of paper on which she had written these words from Robert Browning's poem, 'Rabbi ben Ezra':

Grow old along with me!
The best is yet to be,
The last of life, for which the first was made:
Our times are in His hand,
Who saith, 'A whole I planned,
Youth shows but half; trust God:
See all, nor be afraid!

The octogenarian writer, Professor Paul Rowntree Clifford, includes the same quotation in his remarkable book *Expanding Horizons: Fulfilment in Later Life* (Lion, 1997). If you feel I am something of a whippersnapper to be writing about retirement after experiencing only three months of it, you may wish to consult the much wider experience of Professor Clifford. He knows there are many painful possibilities that make people fear the later years of life – the inevitable diminishing of physical and mental agility, the increasing chance of infirmity and disability, the loss of those near and dear to us.[1] Professor Clifford tells us that he has experienced all these things. And yet he is still able to write, 'As I look back over a long life, I find that old age has been a fulfilment of everything that has gone before, and I would not choose to go back to my youth even if I could do so.'

What lies at the heart of this spirit of positivity and fearlessness, which is so characteristic of people like Paul Clifford and Noel Fletcher, and which makes them affirm with Browning that 'The best is yet to be ... trust God, see all, nor be afraid'? I think there may be three main factors. If we can lay hold of them here and now, they will be an investment that will pay spiritual dividends later on.

The first is the conviction that the Christ who is with us is truly to be trusted. In our early years we have to accept this by an act of faith, but as life goes on we amass personal evidence. Then, whenever we need to do so, we can open the storehouse of memory and know from actual experience what a friend we have had in Jesus over the years. One of the joys of the retirement years is the ability to do just that.

Canon Keith de Berry, formerly Rector of St Aldate's, Oxford, was a great and a good influence on me in my formative student days. Years later, after he had retired, I asked him what was the main truth he had learned during his many years in the ministry. After thinking for a moment, he said just three words, 'He is faithful.' Paul said exactly the same thing: 'The one who calls you is faithful' (1 Thess 5:24). I am sure Noel Fletcher and Paul Clifford would not disagree.

The second factor to encourage a spirit of positivity and fearlessness in life's later years is the widely acknowledged experience that, as the human mind and body age, the human spirit need not do the same. In fact, curiously, it can do the very opposite. Victor Hugo asks the question, 'Why is my soul more luminous as the bodily powers begin to fail? Winter is on my head, but eternal spring is in my heart.' Speaking personally, I believe that Eira and I are getting younger as we get older! Not long ago I was invited to go to a theological college to preach on Psalm 103. It is, I think, my favourite psalm and has a wonderful opening:

> Praise the Lord, O my soul;
>   all my inmost being, praise his holy name.
> Praise the Lord, O my soul,
>   and forget not all his benefits –
> who forgives all your sins
>   and heals all your diseases,
> who redeems your life from the pit
>   and crowns you with love and compassion,
> who satisfies your desires with good things
>   so that your youth is renewed like the eagle's.

As I spoke about these words of the psalmist, I think the students were quite surprised to hear me say that the difference between me in my sixties and me in my teenage years is that I am now much younger than I was then! In fact, it should not have surprised any of us – Jesus teaches that Christian maturity involves an internal process of getting younger: 'Anyone who will not receive the kingdom of God like a little child will never enter it' (Mark 10:15). Anyone who fails to become younger as he or she grows older is to be pitied.

> An aged man is but a paltry thing,
> A tattered coat upon a stick, unless
> Soul clap its hands and sing, and louder sing
> for every tatter in its mortal dress...

W B Yeats[2]

On the other hand, anyone who experiences the rejuvenating power of the Christ who is with us will find that a growing inner youthfulness is considerable compensation for any outward liabilities.

The third and final factor to consider concerns what some find the greatest terror of all – the prospect of death. The ancient world was paralysed by the fear of death. People would undergo various curious rituals in an attempt to take this fear away: for example, the ceremony called *taurobolium* in which someone would lie in a trench and allow the blood of a slaughtered bullock to flow over them while prayers were offered up to the goddess Cybele. Of course these rituals did not work, and people ended up as frightened as ever, if not more so! However, it was widely noticed that the Christian faith had the power to take away the fear of death:

> Man is by nature afraid of death and the dissolution
> of the body, but the remarkable thing is this, that
> when he accepts the faith of the cross, he disregards
> this natural characteristic and through Christ he loses
> his fear of death.
>
> *Athanasius*

We have an older friend, a lovely man and a key member of his local church, who when asked how he is always answers, 'In the departure lounge.' I met him again recently.

'How are you?' I asked.

'Still in the departure lounge,' he replied with a smile.

The flight does not bother him at all, and he has no qualms about its destination.

This sort of relaxed attitude to death can have a marvellously liberating effect on life's closing years. I believe it is well-founded, and I will offer evidence for this in a later chapter. However, for now let me just record my conviction that it is God's will that death, when it comes, should come not as a fiend but as a friend. We are not meant to regard it as the ultimate Terminator. Rather, death is just as an 'attendant' who will escort us into the even closer presence of the One who has been our joy in life and who will be our still deeper joy in the mystery of eternity.

Notes

1 I have written more about facing bereavement in chapter ten of *How to Pray When Life Hurts*.

2 From 'Sailing to Byzantium' in *The Collected Poems of W B Yeats*. Used with permission of A P Watt Ltd on behalf of Michael Yeats.

Chapter 7

THE MIRACLE OF CHRIST WITH US

So far we have been looking at the difference Jesus can make if he is truly with us through all the different stages of life. It is now time for us to ask the question, 'But *how* can this be so? How can I know that as I make my way through this day Jesus will be at my side?'

The concept of 'Christ with us' is a truly extraordinary claim – amazing, presumptuous, and stretching the human mind to and beyond its limit.

Look at it this way. I am a tiny speck on the surface of planet earth. If someone were to give me a globe and ask me to mark myself on it, I could not do it – I am just too small, too insignificant.

Planet earth is itself insignificant in terms of the solar system. If I were to be asked to draw a map of our solar system showing the position of the earth, there is no way I could draw it to scale – the earth is too small. If I were to represent the earth by drawing a circle with a diameter of one inch, the map would have to be so big it would more than cover Greater London!

And if an attempt were made to produce a working model of the known universe showing the position of the solar system, once again there is no way it could be constructed to scale. The solar system is totally insignificant in comparison with the rest of the universe. Once again, if I were to represent the whole solar system by a marble with a diameter of one inch, the model would cover much of England! So the fact of the matter is that I am a tiny speck, on a planet which is a tiny speck, in a solar system which is a tiny speck, in a known universe which is probably a tiny speck in something greater still. And yet I am claiming that the power behind it all has not only taken an interest in our insignificant planet earth but actually also in me! And, more than that, I am claiming that the power behind the universe is with me every moment of every day and night through Jesus!

What colossal cheek! What mind-shattering impertinence!

Just suppose that I were for some curious reason to be filled with a consuming concern for the worms under the lawn outside our house. Suppose by some miracle I were to undergo a metamorphosis in which I actually became a worm and lived among them, taking the risk of some human foot squashing me or a lawnmower blade cutting me in half. That would be nothing compared to what Christians are claiming God has done through Jesus!

And yet much of our nation reacts to this claim with disinterested complacency. 'God became man, did he? That's nice,' we say. 'Let's sing a few Christmas carols about it, and we'll all enjoy the cosy, sentimental feeling we get from them.' Or even worse, 'God became man, did he? How boring. Let's forget about it and concentrate on the really interesting bits of Christmas, like having lots of time off work, and eating and drinking too much, and putting up tinsel and having parties.'

Not that I have anything against carols or Christmas

celebrations. But I can only think that those who react to the Christmas message with sentimentality or boredom have never properly heard the message nor understood it, or if they have heard and understood, have decided they don't believe a word of it. In the rest of this chapter and in the one that follows, I want to try to put in place the basic building blocks on which the incredible Christian doctrine of God's incarnation as man – the amazing concept of 'Christ with us' – is founded.

To begin right at the very beginning, the first of those building blocks is the fact that Jesus is an actual historical person. Don't be put off if you come across the fashionable but ignorant notion that he can be consigned to the world of myth and legend. Jesus walked the dusty roads of Palestine, and if you had been alive two thousand years ago you could have seen his footprints. The evidence for the historicity of Jesus is massive and comes from both Christian and non-Christian sources.

During my days at Manchester Grammar School, and later at Oxford, I was privileged to have a classical education. I spent years studying Latin and Greek texts and life in the ancient world. I remember one day sitting at my desk, wrestling with the angular Latin of the Roman historian Tacitus and suddenly realising, with almost a sense of shock, that he was writing about Jesus – his life, his death and his capacity to attract followers called 'Christians'. It was not that Tacitus had any great regard for Jesus – he seemed to follow the official Roman line of seeing him as something of a nuisance and an oddity. However, he leaves us absolutely no reason to doubt that Jesus existed.

I was subsequently to learn that other Roman authors – Pliny the Younger and Suetonius – also wrote about Jesus, as did the Greek writer Thallus and the Jewish writer Josephus. And, quite apart from the world of ancient literature, we also learn of Jesus from the various inscriptions and graffiti that have been discovered. However, our most extensive source of evidence is the collection of Christian documents we call the New Testament. By any test it is a very impressive record. The reliability and accuracy of ancient documents usually depend on their date and the number and quality of surviving copies. In the case of the historical works of Tacitus we have 20 ancient copies, and the earliest of them can be dated AD1100. By contrast, when we come to the New Testament there are over 24,000 copies, and the earliest full copy can be dated AD350! Moreover, when much of it was being written, there were plenty of eyewitnesses still around to corroborate its truth.

So there is absolutely no doubt whatsoever that Jesus existed. There is also no doubt that he was an enigma to the people of his own time, just as he is an enigma to us today. He is an enigma in two parts. The first is the fact that he was a real man who underwent real experiences and real emotions which could be both positive and negative. At a negative level, he could feel hungry, angry, sad, tired and thirsty (Matt 4:2; Mark 3:5; 14:34; John 11:35; 19:28); he could suffer physically, mentally and spiritually, even to the point of feeling forsaken by God (Mark 15:34). Yet the dominant human picture we have of him is essentially positive. He pulsated with life. He liked a good party and enjoyed a good meal and a drink (John 2:1–11). He was a natural storyteller (Matt 13:34). Rogues and vagabonds found him irresistible (Luke 5:29–30; 7:34), and soldiers were drawn to him because of his straight-talking (Luke 7:2–10). But, for the same reasons, he got right up the noses of politicians and priests.

Now we come to the second half of the enigma. Jesus was certainly man, but he was not *mere* man. He did extraordinary deeds which could not be explained at the time and cannot be explained now. He said extraordinary things and made extraordinary claims: that anyone had only to look at him if they wanted to see God; that all the prophets and teachers of the past had been no more than God's servants, whereas he was God's own eternal Son (John 14:7–11; Heb1:1–3); that he had been in existence before Abraham was born (John 8:58); that, at the end of time, he would return to pass judgement on the whole world (Matt 16:27; John 5:22–23).

What are we to make of someone who says such things? I once knew a man who thought he was God. He was subsequently admitted to a mental hospital. Could Jesus have been mad? I cannot think so. In him there is such unequalled wisdom and sanity.

Could he have been a deliberate liar, manipulating the truth for some selfish and evil purpose of his own? Again, I cannot think so. His whole life, his whole essence, speaks of consummate goodness.

If Jesus is neither mad nor bad, then amazingly and shockingly can he be anything other than what he says he is – the God-Man? That is the enigma.

There suddenly turns up a man who goes about talking as if he was God. He claims to forgive sins. He says he has always existed. He says he is coming to judge the world at the end of time. ... What this man said was, quite simply, the most shocking thing that has ever been uttered by human lips ... I am trying here to prevent anyone saying the really foolish thing that people often say about him: 'I'm ready to accept Jesus as a great moral teacher, but I don't accept his claim to be God.' That is the one thing we must not say. A man who was merely a man and said the sort of things Jesus said would not be a

great moral teacher. He would either be a lunatic –
on a level with the man who says he is a poached
egg – or else he would be the Devil of Hell. You
must make your choice. Either this man was and is
the Son of God: or else a madman or something
worse. You can shut him up for a fool, you can spit
at him and kill him as a demon; or you can fall at his
feet and call him Lord and God. But let us not come
with any patronising nonsense about his being a
great human teacher. He has not left that open to us.
He did not intend to.

C S Lewis[1]

It was a disciple, Thomas – 'Doubting Thomas' we sometimes call him – who first called Jesus, 'My Lord and my
God' (John 20:28). From that time on, the Christian Church
has echoed his words.

In the past God spoke to our forefathers through the
prophets at many times and in various ways, but in
these last days he has spoken to us by his Son, whom
he appointed heir of all things, and through whom he
made the universe. The Son is the radiance of God's
glory and the exact representation of his being...
    [W]hen God brings his firstborn into the world, he
says, 'Let all God's angels worship him.'...
    [A]bout the Son he says, 'Your throne, O God,
will last for ever and ever'...

Hebrews 1:1–3,6,8

It is worth noting just how extraordinary the words spoken
by Thomas, a Hebrew man, were and how extraordinary it
was that they were echoed in a letter designed for readers
who were Hebrews. It would not have been such a shock if

they had been spoken or written in a Roman or Greek context. The Romans were used to the idea that their High God, Jupiter, shared his godhead with other members of the Roman pantheon. The Greek God, Zeus, also shared his godhead with others.

But the God of the Hebrews shared his Godhead with no one. This conviction was absolutely basic to Hebrew life and thought: 'Hear, O Israel: the Lord our God, the Lord is one' (Deut 6:4). Jesus affirmed these words as being amongst the most important in the whole of scripture (Mark 12:28–29). 'You shall have no other gods before me,' thunders the first commandment (Exod 20:3; Deut 5:7). Jesus echoes the thunder: 'Worship the Lord your God, and serve him only' (Matt 4:10; Luke 4:8).

So when the earliest Christians, most of whom were life-long Jews, found themselves worshipping Jesus and were told that the angels worshipped him too, this was for them mind-bending, heart-stopping, soul-blasting stuff. They would never have done it unless their experience of his deeds, his words and his essence left them no option. It went against all their religious conditioning. It also boded ill for their personal survival, because Judaism had been declared a *religio licita* (legal religion) within the Roman empire, whereas once Christianity had made a declaration of independence from its Jewish roots, it was declared a *religio illicita* (illegal religion) and was punishable by death. To worship Jesus Christ was both shocking and highly risky.

Maybe it is time we rediscovered something of the early Christians' sense of shock. When you next celebrate Christmas, by all means read again the lovely stories preserved in the first two chapters of Matthew and Luke, which tell how Jesus came into the world in the little town of Bethlehem, born of a human mother but not a human father;

how he was met by poor shepherds from the nearby hills and by rich strangers from the faraway east; how he was watched not only by representatives of the angelic kingdom, because this was a cosmic event, but also by representatives of the animal kingdom, because he was born in a stable. But as you read these passages, make sure you also look at some of the great interpretative passages from scripture which point out the meaning and the challenge of these events. They shook the foundations of the ancient world, and they can shake the world today if we hear and understand them.

One of the greatest of those passages comes in the first chapter of John's Gospel. Here are the mysterious words (vs1–5,10–14,18):

In the beginning was the Word, and the Word was
with God, and the Word was God. He was with God
in the beginning.

Through him all things were made; without him
nothing was made that has been made. In him was
life, and that life was the light of men. The light
shines in the darkness, but the darkness has not
understood it...

He was in the world, and though the world was
made through him, the world did not recognise him.
He came to that which was his own, but his own did
not receive him. Yet to all who received him, to those
who believed in his name, he gave the right to
become children of God – children born not of
natural descent, nor of human decision or a
husband's will, but born of God.

The Word became flesh and made his dwelling
among us. We have seen his glory, the glory of the
One and Only, who came from the Father, full of
grace and truth.

...No-one has ever seen God, but God the One and Only, who is at the Father's side, has made him known.

This is where John stands. This is his answer to Jesus' own question, 'Who do you say that I am?' (Mark 8:29). For John, Jesus is none other than 'the One and Only' God.

Where do you and I stand? What is our answer when Jesus asks us, 'Who do *you* say that I am?'

Note

1 From C S Lewis, *Mere Christianity*, HarperCollins Publishers Ltd.

Chapter 8

MORE ABOUT THE MIRACLE

In the last chapter we saw that Jesus Christ was undoubtedly a solidly historical person, but he was also an enigmatic one, a real man and yet no *mere* man. We saw that, against all the odds, his followers came actually to worship him.

However, none of this would necessarily guarantee that Christ is with us today. We have put some of the building blocks in place for this doctrine, but not all. There are at least three further things to be considered before you and I can know that we can practise the presence of Christ here and now.

The first is to do with the events that we commemorate every Good Friday. An unholy alliance established between the political and priestly hierarchies of the day, and supported by a baying mob, engineered a death sentence against Jesus. A Roman execution squad did the rest: he was subjected to the agonising and barbaric process of crucifixion. He died horribly. You can read the details in any of the four Gospels, and you might like to take time now to read the account in chapters 14 and 15 of Mark.

However, there was more to all this than met the eye.

The crucifixion was part of Jesus' mission, part of his destiny. He not only came into this world to show us God by the truths he taught and the life he lived; mysteriously, he also came to suffer and to die. He knew this and spoke of it in advance: 'He then began to teach them that the Son of Man must suffer many things and be rejected [and] be killed' (Mark 8:31); '...the Son of Man did not come to be served, but to serve, and to give his life as a ransom for many' (Matt 20:28). It seemed that the Christmas enigma had to deepen, the plot had to thicken.

Most of the ancient world could see no point or purpose in Jesus' death. His own followers were initially horrified at the prospect. When Jesus foretold it, Peter told him off for being morbid, receiving a colossal rebuke in return (Mark 8:32–33), though Jesus himself found the prospect of his death hard to accept (Mark 14:36).

Paul describes the crucifixion as 'a stumbling block to Jews and foolishness to Gentiles' (1 Cor 1:23). A piece of ancient graffiti depicts a kneeling figure worshipping another who is hanging on a cross. The crucified figure has a donkey's head. The caption reads, 'Alexamenos worships his god.' The message? That only a donkey-god would be stupid enough to get himself crucified. And, just to make the pictorial act of ridicule complete, the worshipper is given a donkey's head too!

Yet the crucifixion was not just a sad accident that prematurely terminated a wonderful life: it was a necessary and integral part of that life. Without it, Jesus' work would have been incomplete. One-third of Mark's Gospel deals with the death of Jesus. Can you imagine any other biography spending a third of its pages on its subject's death? On my bookshelf I have Philip Ziegler's biography of Lord Mountbatten who was horrifically murdered by the IRA. But, out of 702 pages, only 4 deal with Mountbatten's death. This is because it was ugly, tragic and served no purpose.

Jesus' death was not like that. It was certainly ugly. It was certainly tragic. But it served an abiding and eternal purpose. Beneath the surface of human nature (and this includes yours and mine) there lurk many horrid things – anger, insecurity, greed, suspicion and more besides. Warm, caring relationships can make a healing difference to us, but this process may involve real risk on the part of the one who is doing the caring. Damaged animals can be dangerous. A friend of mine once took a cat from the animal rescue centre into his home. He carried scratch marks on his hands for weeks afterwards. When I asked him about them, he said, 'You've got to be prepared to bleed a little if you're going to rescue a hurt animal.'

Damaged people are dangerous people. Just imagine for a moment that you have a neighbour who is bitter, twisted and sick in spirit, something of a delinquent, and you care enough to want to help. You would have to offer real friendship, and run the risk of being hurt and rejected. If the door was slammed in your face, you would have to go back again and again. You would have to be prepared to be vulnerable.

Suppose the going got really tough and, in spite of all your friendly approaches, your neighbour was consistently hostile. Say he started threatening you with a knife unless you stayed away, would you or I be 'prepared to bleed a little'? The odds are that we would opt out at that point – most human love has its limits.

But God has no such limitations. His love for delinquent humanity is as infinite as he is himself. As we will see in the next chapter, we are all sinners and the sin within us lashes out at God. Incredibly, in Christ he bears our lash and he bears it to the ultimate degree. On Good Friday he took the worst we could hand out. The Son of God stayed the course with a love that was true to himself, true to his Father and true to our need for salvation. In the mysterious words of the book of Isaiah, written centuries before the event, 'by his wounds we are healed' (Isa 53:5).

So, amazingly, when you and I practise the presence of Christ, we do not have to assume a phoney piety or pretend to possess an unreal righteousness. In the words of Charlotte Elliot's hymn, I can come 'just as I am' and he will pay the price of my coming, and yours too: 'God demonstrates his own love for us in this: While we were still sinners, Christ died for us' (Rom 5:8). This is some love! The love we sing about at Christmas would not have been complete unless Christmas Day had been followed by Good Friday.

Not far from my home is Emmanuel Church, New Brighton. Inside the church, the focal point that the eyes of worshippers are drawn to is a cross with a star above it. There are plans to demolish the present building and to replace it with a new one. If this happens, I hope that the symbolism of the cross and the star will be retained, because if God is to be with us in Christ (and Jesus' title 'Emmanuel' simply means 'God with us') we will need to follow the Christmas star *and* stand at the foot of the cross. Both are necessary and each implies the other.

The miracle of 'Christ with us' was still not complete as the first Good Friday came to an end. An appalling price had to be paid for Christ to be truly with us, the price of life itself: but, having said that, you cannot have a relationship with a corpse. So herein lies the paradox. For Jesus to be with us he had to die. But for us to be with Jesus he has to be alive. In other words, the crucifixion would be a terrible and tragic waste unless somehow subsequently God the Father raised his Son from the dead. And, according to the scriptures, this is exactly what happened (Matt 27:32 – 28:10; Mark 15:21 – 16:8; Luke 24:1–49; John 19:16 – 20:30). Good Friday was followed by Easter Day, when Jesus proved that the power of sin and death could not hold him.

Once again I want to pause and make the point that, like every other part of Jesus' life, the resurrection is firmly embedded in history. Its historicity rests on a mountain of evidence. A solicitor with whom I once discussed the evidence for the resurrection said to me, 'You know, this evidence is so strong that it would certainly convince any court in the land!'

Since then I have noted that many eminent legal figures have gone on record as saying exactly the same thing. For instance, Lord Darling (former Lord Chief Justice of England) wrote of Jesus' resurrection, 'In its favour as a living truth, there exists such overwhelming evidence, positive and negative, factual and circumstantial, that no intelligent jury in the world could fail to bring in a verdict that the resurrection story is true.' And Lord Lyndhurst (former Attorney General of Great Britain) wrote, 'I know pretty well what evidence is and I tell you such evidence as that for the Resurrection has never broken down yet.' So what is this evidence?

There is no lack of non-biblical references to Jesus' resurrection by writers in the eighty years following his death. The Epistle of Barnabas (*circa* AD70) refers to it, as does Flavius Josephus (or perhaps an early interpreter of his writings, *circa* AD94). Others include Clement, Bishop of Rome (AD96–97); Ignatius of Antioch (who died in AD115); and a contemporary of Ignatius, Polycarp, Bishop of Smyrna.

The biblical evidence is earlier still. When Paul writes about Jesus' resurrection appearances (*circa* AD56) to Peter, to all twelve disciples, to a crowd of over five hundred people, to James on his own, to all the apostles, and finally to

Paul himself (1 Cor 15:3–8), he was relying on eye-witnesses. The things he said could be checked and exposed if they were wrong, just as I could be checked if I were to write about life in the second world war. In fact Paul was nearer by far to Jesus' resurrection than we are to the war. And to his letters must be added the evidence of the four Gospels, written later in the same century (only a few years later in the case of Mark).

Contemporaries who denied the Christian interpretation of events seemed not to deny that the tomb was empty and the stone rolled away from the entrance, and this in itself appears to point to the truth of the resurrection. The Christian claim that Jesus had risen from the dead may be hard to believe, but the alternative explanations offered do not bear investigation at all. It is difficult to believe that Jesus' followers would remove his body and then go on to bear witness to and die for a fraud, or that his enemies would steal the body and never think to say so when Christians were claiming a resurrection.

There is further evidence in the fact that Sunday is still observed throughout the world as a holy day nearly two thousand years after the resurrection. Before the first Easter Sunday, Saturday was the Jewish holy day – the Sabbath, the day God himself had designated as *the* special day of the week, set aside for rest and worship (Gen 2:3). The Jews knew that their forefathers had actually died to preserve this day – it was just about as deep an institution as it is possible to conceive.[1] We know how difficult institutions are to change – Oliver Cromwell tried to abolish Christmas in England and failed miserably. You don't get rid of an institution easily.

Yet after Easter Day the early Christians (who at the beginning were mainly Jews) began gradually and naturally to change their holy day to Sunday. It was a momentous and unprecedented change, but it commemorated a momentous and unprecedented event. The day on which Jesus rose from the dead had to be the holiest day of all. The early Christians wanted to leave evidence of this fact, and so they have.

Eye-witnesses, letters, Gospels, the empty tomb, the moving of the stone, the moving of the holy day – this is all powerful evidence. But more powerful still is the fundamental change that took place in Jesus' disciples after the resurrection. From a beaten, bewildered, frightened group who huddled together in an upper room, they were transformed into a purposeful, courageous company whose aim was to conquer the world for Christ. There were thousands of converts. When Christianity was declared an illegal religion and punishable by death, thousands faced martyrdom. What made them do it? They said it was because they knew that Christ was risen and so they did not fear death. Is there any other feasible explanation? I know of none. After many years' experience of ministry, I have learned that human nature is intractable stuff. What other than the miracle of the resurrection could have changed it?

The Christian claim is that after Jesus had been put to death by a Roman execution squad – who certainly knew their gruesome trade – and after his body had been buried in a sealed tomb, God the Father intervened. Jesus' earthly remains could no longer be found, in spite of the fact that the Roman authorities had put a guard on his tomb. But Jesus himself was vibrantly alive. Hundreds of people saw him. Thousands of lives were changed within a few weeks. Millions of lives have been changed since.

Of course, there are many who don't believe a word of this. They take the view that because the whole thing is totally beyond our understanding, because our minds cannot conceive how it could be possible, the resurrection must be rejected, however strong the evidence.

But there is so much we don't understand and yet accept. As I have been writing this chapter, comet Hale Bopp has been clearly visible in the sky above the Wirral. Eira and I have had a splendid view of it from our sitting-room window. We are told that it was last here in the days of ancient Egypt and it won't be back for another 2,400 years. It is travelling at 43,000 miles per hour, and at its closest point to our house it will be 123,000,000 miles away.

But here is a curious thing. Even when I am looking at it, I cannot actually be sure it is still there, because its light takes eleven and a half minutes to reach me. And much of the universe is not just light minutes away, but light years away, hundreds and thousands of light years. In fact, much of the sky I see at night antedates the earthly life of Jesus.

When I was on the phone to our local observatory this morning, I learned that the furthest point in the universe to be seen with the naked eye is the Andromeda Galaxy. It is over two million light years away. If I see it, I am looking back over two million years! In one sense, at a single glance, I can travel back long before the dawn of humankind!

It will not surprise you that I do not understand this. But probably neither will it surprise you that I still accept the fact of the Andromeda Galaxy. It makes sense to acknowledge my own limitations. It makes equal sense to accept help from those who know more than I do. This is true at a scientific level. It is also true at a spiritual level. It is true if I consider the outer spaces of the universe. It is also true if I consider the inner space of the human spirit.

In taking account of spiritual matters I know of no better guide and helper than Jesus himself. In all things connected with the mystery and purpose of life, I find in him unparalleled wisdom and understanding. As far as the resurrection is concerned, he predicted it just as he predicted his crucifixion:

'...the Son of Man will be betrayed to the chief
priests and teachers of the law. They will condemn
him to death and will hand him over to the Gentiles,
who will mock him and spit on him, flog him and
kill him. Three days later he will rise.'

Mark 10:33–34

According to all the evidence, events happened just as Jesus
said they would. It was a mysterious business, but this is a
mysterious universe. We do not understand the half of it.
And if we are right in identifying Jesus as the 'God-Man',
there is a strange, internal logic to it all. You can't keep a
God-Man down! However, there remains yet one more
building block to put in place before the doctrine of 'Christ
with us' can be regarded as complete.

During his earthly life Jesus could not be in two places at
a time. If he was driving the moneychangers out of the temple in Jerusalem, he could not simultaneously be sitting by
the Sea of Galilee, teaching the people. And vice versa. The
same was actually true during the forty days of Easter after
his resurrection. He had a new spiritual body with extraordinary new properties and capabilities. But the recorded
evidence still locates him at no more than one place at a
time. For it to be possible for Christ to be with us all a further miracle was needed. He had to become *omnipresent*.
And this brings us to the wonderful and much neglected
event we call the Ascension.

Think back over the forty days of the first Easter. Jesus
had been crucified. Love had hung upon the cross, nailed
there by our sins. But now he was risen. Love could be put
to death, but could not be held by death. His risen body was
seen here and there. He was vibrantly alive, but his appearances were unpredictable. Then he called his disciples to
the Mount of Ascension (Matt 28:16–20; Acts 1:6–9). The

disciples were bewildered, we are told that some had doubts (Matt 28:17), but their discipleship was stronger than their doubts – Jesus had called them to the Mount and they responded to his call. We are told that Jesus spoke to them of his kingship: 'All authority in heaven and on earth has been given to me' (v18). He gave them, and us, a commission: 'Therefore go and make disciples of all nations, baptising them in the name of the Father and of the Son and of the Holy Spirit, and teaching them to obey everything I have commanded you' (vs19–20). In a moment, the mist would swirl about him and his resurrection body would be taken from their sight (Acts 1:9).

However, he had one final word for them, a final promise, a final gift: 'And surely I am with you always, to the very end of the age' (Matt 28:20). This was the solemn pledge he gave his followers. It always reminds me of one of my favourite quotations, a comment made by the Christian explorer, David Livingstone, as he considered those words of promise on the Mount of Ascension. 'This,' he said, 'is the word of a gentleman of the strictest and most sacred honour, and there's an end on't!'

Ascensiontide is the festival celebrating the omnipresence of Jesus. What a shame and a waste it is that many Christians, though they observe Christmas, Good Friday and Easter, behave as though Ascensiontide did not exist. It is a festival to observe with gratitude and wonder, and its message of 'Christ with us' is one to celebrate and cherish with heart and soul.

In earlier chapters I hope I was able to make the point that the experience of Christ with us can make a radical and transforming difference through all the different stages of life. It is now time to ask the question, what sort of people can realistically expect to benefit from this pledge of Jesus? He will never force himself on anybody, so to whom has the

Christ who has lived, died, risen and ascended, promised to come? Can we know that you and I are among them?

Note
1 It is worth reading 1 Maccabees 2:34–41 in the Apocrypha to understand just how precious the Sabbath was, and how ingrained in the minds and hearts and souls of the people.

Chapter 9

SINNERS WELCOME!

If the God of all Creation has really come to earth in and through Jesus Christ, if he has lived among us and died for us, if he then rose from the dead to be alive and available here and now, what sort of people might we expect him to be calling to himself?

On the grounds that Jesus is 'the same yesterday and today and for ever' (Heb 13:8), we can go back to his historical earthly ministry for an answer. And it was an answer which shocked the religious establishment of his day to the core. In Luke's Gospel we are told, 'the Pharisees and the teachers of the law muttered, "This man welcomes sinners..."' (15:2). Jesus himself said, 'I have not come to call the righteous, but sinners' (Matt 9:13). He told a story to illustrate this point (Luke 18:9–14) and, according to Luke, he told it 'to some who were confident of their own righteousness and looked down on everybody else' (v9).

Two men go into the temple to pray. One of them is a Pharisee with an impressive track record of public and personal piety. The other is one of the hated tax collectors working for the Roman occupying power, squeezing money out of the people, some for the authorities and some for their own pockets. They are regarded as quislings and cheats.

So apparently we have a good guy and a bad guy here. The 'good guy' is distinctly pleased with his own goodness, and parades his track record before God. He is, he says, grateful to be so much better than others: 'I am not like other men – robbers, evildoers, adulterers – or even like this tax collector' (v11). We can imagine his disdainful gesture as he says the words. He goes on to remind God that he fasts twice a week and gives him a tenth of his income. Pretty good, hey? He certainly thinks so. For there he ends his prayer.

By contrast, the tax collector, the 'bad guy', is far from pleased with himself. He realises that his way of life leaves much to be desired. He finds a quiet place right at the back of the temple. He cannot raise his eyes from the ground. He actually hits himself physically as he reproaches himself for the faults he finds in his life. As for his prayer, all that he can bring himself to say is 'God, have mercy on me, a sinner' (v13).

Jesus tells us the point of the story. Two men have said their prayers, but only one of them ends up in a true relationship with God. A right relationship with him requires insight and perspective. And in a world gone wrong, a spirit of repentance is an essential part of that insight and perspective. The tax collector has this spirit of repentance, the Pharisee does not. Thus, paradoxically, it is the 'good guy' who ends up estranged from God, and the 'sinner' who receives God's welcome.

If you and I have any sort of insight into ourselves, this is good news for us because 'all have sinned and fall short of the glory of God' (Rom 3:23). That includes you and me

– we are part of a flawed species which has made a fundamental error. This error is to put self at the centre of life, in the place that God alone should occupy.

The Bible graphically presents the basic problem of human nature in the story of the Fall (Gen 2–3). Adam (Hebrew for 'mankind') is created by God. To ensure that human life may continue, God creates Eve (Hebrew for 'life'). The man and woman are placed together in the garden of Eden (Hebrew for 'delight'). To remain in this garden of delight, all that is necessary is that they undertake a small symbolic act of obedience to acknowledge God as their source and centrepoint – they are to avoid the fruit on just *one* of the trees in the garden. No big deal, you would have thought.

But at this point 'the serpent' (symbol of the devil, the power of evil) enters the scene. The serpent ensures that Adam and Eve start to want the one thing they cannot have. The words he tempts them with are very significant: '*Be like God*,' he hisses (Gen 3:5) – in other words, 'Put self in the centre of life where God should be'. He offers them not just a theological do-it-yourself kit but a theological be-it-yourself kit. And they fall for the temptation and lose their place in the garden of delight.

'Be like God – put self at the centre of life.' We still fall for it. I think the first time I was really struck by the universality of human self-centredness was during my National Service days when I was stationed for a time at Normanton Barracks, Derby. There was a passage linking two of the main roads in Derby. I did not have to go along it but often had to walk past one end, and that passage started to intrigue me. About halfway down it, there was a point at which everybody who was walking along looked at the wall. Some stopped and stared in a fairly deliberate fashion; others just flicked an almost guilty glance over one shoulder. I never saw anyone ignore it.

I wondered what could be of such interest to absolutely everybody. In the end my curiosity got the better of me. I went down the passage to see what was on the wall. Can you guess? Retrospectively, I reckoned I could have worked it out if I had thought about it sufficiently. Most interests are partial and sectional. For instance, if there had been a pornographic drawing or poster on the wall, some people would have stopped and slavered over it while others would have turned away. But there is one thing we are *all* interested in – ourselves. It was a mirror!

Just check yourself. Suppose someone were to come to you at this moment with a group photo taken at work or at church or at some club you belong to, and you are one of the group. Whose face would you look for first?

You may think this sort of self-centredness is a very small thing compared to the real problems of the world like, for example, the growth of violent crime which threatens the peace of society, or the abandonment of traditional sexual morality which threatens the health of society, or the many instances of ecological irresponsibility which could actually threaten life on earth. However, violent crime stems from the self-centred notion that *my* desires are more important than the rights of others; sexual immorality stresses *my* gratification and treats others as the means to that end; and in ecological irresponsibility *my* greed takes precedence over the well-being of the planet.

In other words, self-centredness is a sort of Pandora's box. Open it and out come the ills of the world. When self-centredness becomes the norm, the garden of delight can turn into a chamber of horrors. In the Genesis story, once Adam and Eve fall for the serpent's temptation and put self in the place God should have, everything starts to go wrong. They become alienated from their own inner selves (Gen 3:7), alienated from God (v8) and alienated from each other (v12). They become alienated from the ground under their feet (v17) and from any prospect of life at its fullest and best (v24). They transmit this sense of alienation to their sons, one of whom murders the other (4:8). Self-centredness causes trouble, trouble and yet more trouble.

The most serious thing is the power that our self-centred sinfulness has to alienate us from God. God is the source of life: to be separated from him is to be separated from life. This would be bad enough if there were no more to us than our years here on earth. But if, as I shall be urging in the next chapter, we are designed to explore eternity, then the pain and the waste can hardly be imagined. Sin is a serious business. The human experience is a matter of life and death, and 'the wages of sin is death' (Rom 6:23).

And yet mysteriously Jesus has collected our lethal pay-packet. If we accept relationship with him, for which he has paid the price of death on the cross, he offers a way back to God the Father, a right attitude to our neighbours and the rediscovery of inner peace. This is the good news for sinners.

It is as though Jesus carries two placards. One bears the words 'DOWN WITH SIN' – sin spoils life and threatens survival both here and in eternity. But the other carries the words 'UP WITH SINNERS' – sinners though we are, we are rich in potential and infinitely precious to God.

Of course, this is not good news for us if we do not know we are sinners. In the story of the Pharisee and the tax collector, it was good for the tax collector who knew he was a sinner, but not for the Pharisee who regarded himself with total self-satisfaction. Nor is there good news for any modern-day equivalent of the Pharisee.

Some years ago, when I was a part-time hospital chaplain and in the process of going round a ward, having a few words with each patient, I remember coming across a man who waved me aside with the words, 'Don't bother coming to me. I have no need and no use for the church. I set myself much higher standards than those of the Christian church, and I have never ever disappointed myself yet.'

I took out my notebook and asked, 'Do you mind if I write your words down?' I wrote, 'I set myself much higher standards than those of the Christian church, and I have never ever disappointed myself yet.'

I promised him I would think about what he had said and asked if, in turn, I might give him something to consider. Taking his copy of *The Guardian*, I wrote in the margin: 'If we claim to be without sin, we deceive ourselves and the truth is not in us' (1 John 1:8). I have to admit that he hardly looked impressed and I wonder if he ever got round to thinking about these words. I know I went away feeling very sad.

You will not find any relevance in the Saviour if you reckon there is absolutely nothing you need to be saved from. But sinners who know they are sinners are welcome in the Lord's presence. Mind you, we have to be sinners who are prepared to change. This life-change is never a condition of our coming to Jesus, but it is an *inevitable consequence* if our coming is real. Mary Magdalene certainly found this to be so, as did the apostle Paul (Luke 8:1–2; Acts 9) and later Augustine of Hippo (AD354–430). This is how Augustine describes his early pre-Christian life and the contrast of the life that followed his discovery of Christ:[1]

I took my fill of hell. I ran wild in a rank forest of shady amorous adventures ... Out of the slimy potholes of the flesh there arose vapours that exhaled upon and covered over and obscured my heart ... I was tossed back and forth, spilling, squandering, and wasting in my fornicating ... The companions with whom I tramped the streets were certainly nothing to boast about. We reeled and wallowed about in the filth, as though it were expensive perfume!

But you put a halt to that and confirmed your way to me, telling me that since Christ died for all men, those who live should no longer live to themselves, but to him who died for all. So, Lord, I am casting all my cares on you, that I may live and consider wondrous things out of your law. You know my weakness and my ignorance; teach me and make me whole. Your only Son, in whom are hid all the treasures of wisdom and knowledge, has redeemed me with his blood.

Augustine went on to become one of the great saints and theologians of the Christian church.

If that seems a startling contrast, transformations just as great still happen around us today. As I write, three people come to mind. The first is David Hamilton, a Northern Irishman who used to be a terrorist in the UVF (the Ulster Volunteer Force, an illegal loyalist paramilitary organisation). He was a man of violence, whose hands were stained with blood. And those bloodstains seemed destined to grow because he had drawn up a death-list of people he had sworn to kill. Then he became a committed Christian and his life changed completely.

It was a risky business. He had to tell those over him in the UVF that in future he felt he must be a man of the Bible, not a man of the bullet. For a time it was uncertain whether he would be executed as a deserter and a coward. But, to his relief, it was decided that unless it were subsequently to appear that his conversion was not genuine, he would be allowed to leave the UVF without penalty.

But the risks were not over. An IRA terrorist had David

on his own death-list. Shortly after David's conversion, the two of them came face to face.

'I hear you're a Christian now,' said the IRA man, 'so you can't shoot back any more.'

'That's right,' David admitted. The next moment, to his amazement, he was in the other man's arms. The IRA terrorist had become a Christian too!

David Hamilton is now a full-time worker for Teen Challenge, a Christian group that seeks to help troubled young people. Before I retired from my last parish, he came over to speak to our congregation. You could have heard a pin drop as he told the story of his life and the difference Christ has made in it.[2]

No less startling is the story of Nigel Holme. He was abused as a child, and perhaps that abuse motivated his subsequent decision to pioneer the nation's first telephone sex chat-line. It was a sleazy but lucrative occupation, and Nigel became a rich man. But he was not a happy one, and he squandered both his money and his health on alcohol. Then, in 1991, he became a Christian. He now runs the National Christian Helpline (tel 0345 056064). Recently, in an absorbing and challenging interview on BBC Radio Merseyside, he told the story of his life and of the difference Jesus has made to him.

As a further illustration of the life-transforming power of Jesus, what about Bobby Ball of the well-known Cannon and Ball comedy duo? Coming, as he did, from a simple and basic northern background, Bobby found success and wealth hard to deal with. He gained a big house, a sizeable bank-balance, a Rolls Royce and top billing on the stage and television. But as his career was on the way up, his personal life was on the way down. By his own admission, he became a thoroughly unpleasant person. He lost the friendship of his comedy partner, Tommy Cannon. They stayed together on the stage for the sake of the money they were making, but off-stage they hardly spoke. He almost lost his wife Yvonne – his drinking, violence and infidelity put a tremendous strain on their marriage. He also lost his personal happiness and peace of mind.

Then, to everybody's amazement, he became a Christian. Tommy's reaction was that now, on top of everything else, his partner had gone mad! However, gradually those around Bobby started to see signs of a welcome change in him. Six months later Yvonne became a Christian too. Tommy took longer. It was eight years before he made a Christian commitment himself. Now, after thirty-five years together, Tommy and Bobby's partnership is stronger than ever and their friendship has been renewed. They have a new aim – not just to share their humour but also to share their Christian faith. As I write, they have embarked on a national tour with a unique chat show called *An Audience with Cannon and Ball*, and a fortnight before I wrote this chapter they came to our local theatre, the Floral Pavilion at New Brighton. Eira and I went along to see the show.

It began with an hour of vintage Cannon and Ball comedy as they told the story of their early life and times. Then, to the surprise of some in the audience, they both spoke of their new-found Christian faith and invited questions and comments from the audience. Some reacted with hostility. One man said that he objected to the religious turn the show had taken – he had come for a laugh not a sermon!

Bobby Ball patiently pointed out that nothing had been misrepresented on the posters which advertised 'Bobby and Tommy in a non-stop celebration of 35 years in showbusiness, singing and chatting their way through their life, their work *and their faith*.'

Another man suggested that this might be just another clever way to make money. Bobby answered that they were actually making nothing out of this tour at all. It was just their way of trying to give something back to the Lord who had given them so much.

Then a woman nervously said she was a Roman Catholic, but she did not understand what they meant by a 'committed, born-again Christian'. Bobby explained that it was just what happens to you when you accept God's forgiveness and start to walk through life with Jesus at your side. The show finished with a song, and the audience went home.

I wonder what they made of it all. I wonder if anyone found faith for the first time. One thing was certain. Nobody could have doubted that Tommy Cannon and Bobby Ball were changed men.

Where does the change come from when sinners like Augustine of Hippo, David Hamilton, Nigel Holme, Bobby Ball, Tommy Cannon and – please God – ourselves are welcomed into the presence of Jesus and begin to discover what it means to have Christ with us?

Our own will-power has a part to play, but it is a small part. We are asked to provide our active consent and our active co-operation. But the actual resources for the change are to be found elsewhere.

People are always influenced by the company they keep, and there can be no better example of this than the transforming friendship of Jesus himself. The experience of Christ with us is never a non-event. There is so much that he pours from his generous heart into ours that we just have to be changed and become channels of it.[3] Where Jesus is, there too is the whole might of the Holy Trinity. Jesus himself said, 'Anyone who has seen me has seen the Father' (John 14:9). So, as we encounter Jesus, we also encounter the Father's creative and re-creative power. And, in the words of the Nicene Creed, 'proceeding from the Father and the Son' comes the Holy Spirit, the God within, whom Jesus promised to his followers (John 14:26). The Holy Spirit is rich in fruit, generous in gifts and dynamic in impact. But his work is a mystery and a miracle requiring a whole book to itself. All that need be said here is that the resources available for our Christian journey are no less than those of God the Father, God the Son and God the Holy Spirit. All these resources are offered to us in and through the Christ who promised to be with us if we invite him to be. But God is a gentleman. Jesus is no gatecrasher. He stands at the door of our life and knocks: we will only know his presence if we open the door (Rev 3:20).

It may be helpful if at this point I include a prayer of response to Jesus which, if you choose to, you can take a moment to say. I have included it in several of my books, and many people have told me how much it has meant to them. It can be used as an initial act of assent to the Christian faith or as a way of affirming and deepening a faith that is already there:

> Jesus, I know I am a sinner, and I am truly sorry for the wrongs I have done. But I also know that you love me and gave yourself for me. You offer to come into my life if I will let you. You offer healing for the sins and hurts of my soul. You offer to feed me with your own truth.
>
> Gratefully I accept your offer to be my Saviour, Lord and friend. I ask for your forgiveness. I put my trust in you and want you to work in me, healing me, feeding me, living in me.
>
> Help me to use my life in your service. Thank you for all you are going to do in me. Amen.

If you believe this is a good and appropriate prayer for you, then I suggest that you go ahead and actually pray it. Don't just read it and put it aside for a more suitable or more formal time of prayer. We are great procrastinators, we human beings. We are expert in putting things off. We duck and weave and delay. But if a thing is worth doing, it's worth doing *now*.

Before this chapter comes to an end, here are a couple of quotations to focus our minds. The first is a poem by Henry Twells, which is inscribed on a clock in Chester Cathedral:

> When, as a child, I laughed and wept,
> Time crept.
> When, as a youth, I dreamt and talked,
> Time walked.
> When I became a full grown man,
> Time ran.
> When older still I daily grew,
> Time flew.
> Soon I shall find, on travelling on,
> Time gone.
> O Christ, wilt thou have saved me then?

And, for the second, this bleak reminder from Pam Weaver:

> Many of those who plan to become Christians at the eleventh hour die at 10.30!

Notes

1 From *Confessions*, Sherwood Eliot Wirt (tr).

2 David Hamilton's story is told in the video *The Dividing Wall*, Scripture Union, 1986.

3 This is a theme I have explored in some detail in my
last book *Make me a Channel*, Scripture Union, 1996.

Chapter 10

LIFE THAT IS STRONGER
THAN DEATH

We have almost finished our journey together, but if this book is to be complete there is one further experience we should consider. Though many people are too fearful to think about it directly, it comes to us all sooner or later. So let's face it now.

Because we are all physically finite, we are all inexorably working our way towards our moment of death. We do not know when it will happen, we do not know where it will happen, we do not know how it will happen. But unless the second coming of Jesus happens first, your death and my death is an absolute certainty. So, if we are realists, it makes sense to think about the prospect in advance. In terms of this book, it must be right not only to look death in the eye but also, simultaneously, to look Jesus in the eye and to consider the nature of the difference Christ can make to us at the moment of death and in whatever may lie beyond. I am aware that there is some degree of presumption in dealing with this subject at all. But, nevertheless, it would be cowardly to omit it – so here goes!

First, let me say plainly, in the words of the Nicene Creed, that 'I believe in ... the life of the world to come'. I believe that death is not the great terminus at the end of the human journey nor the fearsome guillotine that cuts away the thread of our existence. Death is more like a gateway, beyond which, I believe, there is a road to travel, a mystery to be explored, an adventure that beckons.

Why do I believe this? Let me attempt a fairly detailed answer. It contains all sorts of ingredients, and it may be helpful if I list them point by point so that you can take your time in thinking about each in turn.

•

It seems to me that the concept of eternal life is actually required by the very nature of the Christian doctrine of God the Father. If the Father is both almighty and all-loving, it would seem logical that nothing he deems to be of value within his creation can ever be wasted. Such a waste would be an affront both to his goodness and his power. So, since he has certainly shown us, through all he has done in Jesus Christ, that he regards each one of us as being of value, it would seem that God has more in mind for you and me than an insignificant and miniscule place on the scrap heap of time.

Even when we waste so much of our own potential through our sin and our folly, his policy is not one of waste disposal but rather of reclamation. Sometimes when I am on holiday and not too keen to be known as a vicar, I tell other guests who ask what my job is that I am in the reclamation business! I reckon it is a fair description of any form of Christian ministry, because the whole of the Bible is a description of God's reclamation programme for the errant and self-destructive human race. And if God is self-consistent and 'does not change like shifting shadows' (James

1:17), there is no way in which that policy and that programme can change at the point of our physical death.

•

If the concept of life after death is required by the doctrine
of God the Father, it seems also to be required by the doctrine of God the Holy Spirit. If God the Holy Spirit is eternal and we are called both to experience him and become
one with him, then it would seem that those who are in any
way invaded by his life and irradiated by his being must
have something of his eternity in them.

•

Indeed, there is something in our own inner life that speaks
of eternity. I suppose this is not surprising if we are made
'in the image of God' (Gen 1:27). Speaking personally, I am
well aware that my physical and mental faculties are subject
to the process of ageing, but I also know there is something
in me – my inner spirit, the essence of the person I am –
which need not and should not suffer the same subjection.
We have already considered this in chapter six, where I
quoted some memorable words of Victor Hugo. Let me
repeat them now in a fuller form:

> You say that the soul is nothing but the resultant of
> bodily powers. Why then is my soul more luminous
> as the bodily powers begin to fail? Winter is on my
> head, but eternal spring is in my heart. The nearer I
> approach the end, the plainer I hear round me the
> immortal symphonies of the world to come.

•

Humankind seems to have felt some sense of the immortal from the very dawn of history. Archaeology and ancient literature are both witness to this. One of the earliest facts known about Stone-age man is that he often buried his dead with valuable tools, weapons and cooking utensils. Stone was used for sepulchres long before it was used for houses. As man became vocal and coherent, he pondered and elaborated on that conviction, and this is reflected in the great ancient religions and philosophies – the elaborate Egyptian death rituals, the Chinese concept of ancestor worship, the Japanese two-tiered afterlife, Hinduism and the imperishable soul or *atman*, Buddhism with its noble eightfold path leading to *nirvana*, the Homeric concept of Hades, the Hebraic idea of Sheol, Plato's teaching on immortality, and so on.

Where does it come from, this ingrained conviction that death is not the end, that beyond lies continued life? Not, one would think, from wishful thinking. There is nothing desirable, for instance, about the Homeric Hades. Total oblivion would be much better.

•

Maybe this conviction is linked to the strange fact that though body, mind and spirit are usually intertwined and interdependent in this life, this does not appear to be inevitably the case. There is certainly a great deal of supporting evidence for the idea that the soul can come 'out of the body'. Many years ago there was a survey of 350 students at Oxford University and it was discovered that 34% claimed they had had out-of-the-body experiences. Subsequently, during the course of my pastoral ministry several people have shared such experiences with me.

Roger, a solid and unemotional university lecturer, told

me that once, while lecturing to a group of students, he found himself somehow separated from his body, looking down upon the class from the back of the room. With a real effort of will he pulled himself back into his body and the lecture continued without a break. As far as he could tell, his students did not notice anything at all.

This sort of experience seems not to come to any one particular personality-type. Gwendoline was a fragile and deeply spiritual Christian woman who, in a time of illness, asked God for relief from her pain. She then found herself hovering above her own body, totally free from any discomfort. She was not at all pleased when at that moment a visitor came to see her and, out of sheer good manners, she felt she had to haul herself back into her suffering body!

The point of including phenomena such as these in a list of factors pointing to life after death is that if there is no necessary junction of body and soul at every moment in this life, then it is not logically necessary to suppose that the soul must cease to exist when the body comes to its end.

•

In fact, out-of-the-body experiences seem characteristically to occur at or around the point of physical death. A whole new 'science' known as thanatology is coming into being to consider these and other edge-of-death experiences.

One of my former parishioners, Donovan, told me about his own experience. Following an operation in one of our local hospitals, it actually appeared that he 'died' for a while. The first thing he knew about it was when he found himself floating above his own body, looking down on it. He discovered he could in fact float away from his body and visit other parts of the hospital. He went into the room where his wife was sitting and listened to some of the things a doctor was telling her about his own operation. Then he returned to the post-operative recovery room where his body was, and was intrigued to find the medical staff in a state of some agitation. 'He's gone!' said one of them.

Donovan is a naturally mischievous person. Concentrating upon his body, as he hovered above it, he suddenly made it cough. The medics leapt upon it, there was a frenzy of resuscitation activity, and almost with a sense of indignity Donovan found himself drawn back into his body. He told me the story afterwards when I visited him in his home, and he included the fact that he subsequently made a point of checking the details of the conversation he had overheard between the doctor and his wife while he was on his travels. It had all happened just as he had heard and seen it.

Reports of edge-of-death experiences sometimes include more than a jaunt around a hospital. Some claim it is possible to leave this earth altogether. Captain Edmund Wilbourne of the Church Army has gone public about an experience of this sort. He has talked about it on local and network radio, and accepted an invitation to preach in my church and answer questions from my congregation. He stayed overnight at our vicarage, so I was able to put many questions of my own to him.

He told us that while he was in a hospital near Manchester, ill with pneumonia and pleurisy, there had been a medical crisis and he was pronounced clinically dead. His body was actually taken to the hospital mortuary. Like Donovan, he began his out-of-the-body experience with a period spent in the hospital premises, during which he watched a young nurse laying out and shaving his body. But, unlike Donovan, his experience did not end there.

After a time he felt as though the cord that had bound him to this world was severed. He found himself in another place, a place of intense light, where he was enfolded by beauty and love. It was, he said, more like a bustling city than a lonely country scene. He was surrounded by people, some of whom he recognised – his mother, his grand-mother, a Sunday School teacher called Frank who had influenced him a great deal but who had lost his life in the second world war, and a saintly Roman Catholic doctor who had just died. He also said that he met Jesus, who in that place of light was 'light itself', who looked at him with eyes that were never to be forgotten. It was, he said, 'a searching look which saw every part of me, but I realised that he could not take his eyes off me because he loved me so.' They talked and laughed together, and as they did so he heard a whisper which became progressively louder. It was the voice of an elderly woman praying, 'O God, don't let him die! He has work to do for you.' It was at this point that he found himself sitting on the mortuary slab – to his own disappointment and to the absolute horror of the mortuary attendant! It turned out that his elderly landlady had been praying this exact prayer at the time.[1]

It should be said that many writers are more sceptical about edge-of-death experiences. In their book *Is there Life After Death?* John Weldon and Zola Levitt warn against the danger of wishful thinking, psychological aberration, and even demonic deception. All we can do here is to consider the evidence – which is certainly plentiful – and then reach our own conclusions.

•

Just as Edmund Wilbourne claimed to have crossed the boundary between time and eternity and back again, it appears that others may have made the trip in the opposite direction. There are solemn warnings in the Bible that the living should never seek contact with the dead (Deut 18:10–12; Isa 8:19–20). However, many say that this contact may take place spontaneously and without any kind of seeking. There is the celebrated instance in which J B Phillips says he was twice visited by C S Lewis after his death (*Ring of Truth*, pp89–90). And among people I have met myself are Bernard, a widower, who told me his wife had visited him in clearly visible form on half a dozen occasions; and Judith, a widow, who said that her husband had come to her several times after his death in a form that was not only visible but tangible, before leaving to explore eternity in the company of his Lord – for he was a deeply committed Christian.

•

Some people do not need to leave their bodies or have a visitor from the next world in order to be convinced they have caught the flavour of eternity. It is more than enough for them that they have had what is usually termed a 'mystic' experience. Over fifty such experiences have been researched and analysed in a scholarly little book by Basil Douglas-Smith, entitled *The Mystics Come to Harley Street* (Regency Press, 1983). I do recommend it.

Of course, for Christians, one of the definitive descriptions of a mystic experience is to be found in 2 Corinthians 12:2–4:

> I know a man in Christ who fourteen years ago was
> caught up to the third heaven. Whether it was in the
> body or out of the body I do not know – God knows.
> And I know that this man – whether in the body or
> apart from the body I do not know, but God knows –
> was caught up to paradise. He heard inexpressible
> things, things that man is not permitted to tell.

Paul speaks in the third person here, but it is usually thought that he is describing his own experience.

•

So far we have looked at a hotch-potch of considerations, some Christian, some non-Christian, some rather trivial, some too deep for words. I believe that in all of this we have come across some strong pointers to the existence of life after death. But for the Christian there are two further massive considerations which, as far as I am concerned, clinch the matter once and for all.

One is the mysterious fact of Jesus' resurrection. We have dealt with it in detail in chapter eight, so nothing more need be said here. Christ is risen and it is his will to share his resurrection life with *us*.

•

Along with the mystery of Jesus' resurrection, we have his plain teaching about life after death. Time and time again archaeology, history, religion, literature and human experience both normal and paranormal hint of the existence of life after death – but Jesus speaks plainly about it. He is not preoccupied with it, but it is an essential strand in his basic teaching. This is recorded by all four Gospel writers. For example, Matthew records Christ's injunction to 'store up for yourselves treasures in heaven' (Matt 6:20); Mark records the promise that those who make sacrifices for the sake of Christ will receive 'in the age to come, eternal life' (Mark 10:30); Luke tells us that the children of the resurrection 'can no longer die; for they are like the angels. They are God's children' (Luke 20:36); and John preserves for us the assurance that 'God so loved the world that he gave his one and only Son, that whoever believes in him shall not perish but have eternal life' (John 3:16).

If you wish to study Jesus' teaching on life after death in greater detail, you may find it helpful to look up these further texts: Mark 12:18–27 (Jesus refutes the Sadducees when they deny the resurrection); John 14:2 (he promises 'many rooms' in the Father's house where he is going ahead to prepare a place for those who follow him); Matthew 13:24–30,36–43 (the parable of the wheat and the weeds); Matthew 25:31–46 (the parable of the sheep and the goats); John 11:25–26 ('I am the resurrection and the life').

Jesus taught about life after death throughout his years of ministry, and he continued to do so even in the hour of his death, when he turned to the penitent thief and said, 'Today you will be with me in paradise' (Luke 23:43).

After this long excursus, what I am saying is that, in the last analysis, I rest in the word of Jesus. Wherever I can test his word, it always rings true. Where I cannot altogether test his word, it seems to me to be right and reasonable to trust him – he has never let me down yet, and I do not believe he is about to let me down in the mysterious issue of eternal life.

However, though I believe firmly in life after death, I ought to say that I do not believe in the concept of automatic heaven for everyone. Oh, I would love to believe it! But it would be neither scriptural nor logical. Jesus teaches that there are two ultimate possibilities for you and me. One is glorious beyond our imagination, the other too horrible to contemplate. He told a story to illustrate the contrast (Luke16:19–31).

There was a beggar called Lazarus who had a hard time in life. He was hungry. He was sick. He was covered in sores. He scavenged for food amongst the garbage outside the house of a rich man.

The rich man did not care about Lazarus. He dressed himself in imperial purple, and only used the finest linen. He lived in luxury every day.

Then both men died. And the beggar was right with God, whereas the rich man was not. The rich man had a fine burial, but it was the beggar who was carried to heaven by the angels.

'In hell, where he was in torment, the rich man
looked up and saw Abraham far away, with Lazarus
by his side. So he called to him, "Father Abraham,
have pity on me and send Lazarus to dip the tip of
his finger in water and cool my tongue, because I am
in agony in this fire."

'But Abraham replied, "Son, remember that in
your lifetime you received your good things, while
Lazarus received bad things, but now he is comforted
here and you are in agony. And besides all this,
between us and you a great chasm has been fixed, so
that those who want to go from here to you cannot,
nor can anyone cross over from there to us." '

And these are the words of 'gentle Jesus'!

We are told that though it is the joy of God to welcome repentant sinners into heaven, nonetheless, those who exclude love from their hearts also exclude the possibility of real life both in time and in eternity. To those who are loveless and therefore lifeless, Christ will say, 'Depart from me, you who are cursed, into the eternal fire prepared for the devil and his angels. For I was hungry and you gave me nothing to eat, I was thirsty and you gave me nothing to drink, I was a stranger and you did not invite me in, I needed clothes and you did not clothe me, I was sick and in prison and you did not look after me' (Matt 25:41–43).

Why must there be two possibilities – life and death, bliss and torment? Not because God is vindictive: God 'wants all men to be saved and to come to a knowledge of the truth' (1 Tim 2:3–4). But listen – 'O Jerusalem, Jerusalem ... how often have I longed to gather your children together, as a hen gathers her chicks under her wings, but you were not willing' (Luke 13:34).

The stumbling block is not in God but in us. Humankind has been created free. Thanks to Jesus, in spite of all our sinfulness, we are free to find a way back to God. We are also free, if we are foolish enough, to choose the road to hell, to reject God and the things of God, selfishly to curl in upon ourselves, almost like some great ingrowing toenail, hurting ourselves, diminishing ourselves and, finally, destroying ourselves. We create and perpetuate hell on earth again and again, exercising our bitter freedom to reject God in Christ. Logically, we must be free to do so in eternity also.

'Do not be deceived,' says Paul, 'God cannot be mocked. A man reaps what he sows. The one who sows to please his sinful nature, from that nature will reap destruction; the one who sows to please the Spirit, from the Spirit will reap eternal life' (Gal 6:7–8).

There is an old saying: 'Take care, O man, on what you set your heart. For you shall surely have it!' This has to be seen not just in the context of time but also of eternity. Man has a basic choice – to go with or against God, to be with or without God. The Christian faith inexorably places the choice before us and leaves us to make our own decision.

The good news is that for those who travel with Jesus there is *nothing* to fear. If we put our hand in his, he leads us through this life in all its different stages, and personally I know of nothing better in this world than to walk through life with him. Then, when we come to the point of death, the promise of the gospel is that he will not pull his hand away. He will take a firm grasp on us and lead us the way he has already gone, into death and through death, into the mystery that lies beyond death. The Christian conviction – grounded in scripture and affirmed by everything we know of the Christ who is with us – is that wherever we travel with Jesus, in this world or the next, we can travel without fear. Instead we can travel with hope, with optimism and, indeed, with the positive expectation that the best is yet to be.

If I may indulge in one more edge-of-death story. Matthew went into hospital for an operation, but something went wrong in the operating theatre. For a few minutes his life hung in the balance. He actually seemed to 'die' for a time but was eventually resuscitated.

When he returned to consciousness, he had quite a story to tell. He stopped me outside church one day, told me of his experience and asked me to pass it on to others.

It seemed to him that he was floating in space. Around him were people he had known during his life. Desperately he tried to hold onto them, but each in turn eluded his grasp. It was then, said Matthew, that Jesus came to him and he knew he was safe: 'I did not need to try to hold onto Jesus. *He held me.*'

We have already considered the total certainty Paul had that absolutely nothing in death or life can separate us from the love of Jesus. Look back to the quotation from Romans 8 at the end of chapter one, and let the words point you again to the power and the wonder of the Christ whose will it is to be with us not only in this life but forever, eternally holding us to himself.

In one sense it is totally beyond us: 'No eye has seen, no ear has heard, no mind has conceived what God has prepared for those who love him' (1 Cor 2:9). And yet in another sense it starts now. Have you noticed how often the present tense is used in the Bible to describe eternal life?

Jesus said, 'He who believes *has* everlasting life' (John 6:47). And John affirms this: 'God has given us eternal life, and this life is in his Son. He who has the Son has life: he who does not have the Son of God does not have life. I write these things to you who believe in the name of the Son of God so that you may know that you have eternal life' (1 John 5:11–13).

It would seem that though our destiny under God is an unfathomable wonder to our finite and mortal minds, nonetheless there are clues everywhere. Here and now the mystery can begin to unfold. Eternity stirs in us and around us. There are glimpses of glory, hints of heaven, foretastes of the banquet to come.

Thomas Traherne once wrote, 'We need nothing but open eyes to be ravished like the Cherubims.' But those eyes must be fixed on Jesus, 'the author and perfecter of our faith' (Heb 12:2). For all these things come with the Christ who himself came to be with us. His will and purpose, in the extraordinary words of Athanasius, is to 'share our humanity, so that we might share his divinity'.

Note

1 If you wish to read a story like this in greater detail, Dr George Ritchie has written of when he too was pro- nounced medically dead from double lobar pneumonia, but mysteriously lived to tell the tale of his out-of-the- body experiences in and beyond this world. He does so in his book *Return from Tomorrow*, Kingwsay, 1978.

Epilogue

THE ROAD TO EMMAUS

They were not a happy couple, the two on the road to Emmaus (Luke 24:13–35).

They had been shattered by the events of the first Good Friday. The one who had been such a source of hope and inspiration had been betrayed, arrested, violated and executed. His broken and blood-spattered body had been taken down from the cross and buried in a tomb. It was horrible.

They could not even count on being left to grieve in peace. Jesus' body had disappeared and the air was rife with incredible rumours. A group of women who had been close to Jesus seemed to be talking absolute nonsense. What were they to believe?

They just wanted to get away from it all, and so they were trudging back from Jerusalem to their home village of Emmaus. The seven-mile journey could never have seemed longer.

We know the name of one of them – he was called Cleopas. We are not told the name of the other. It may possibly have been Mrs Cleopas, unacknowledged because women received scant recognition in Palestinian society. That one of the travellers has no name may, however, be a help to us – we can put ourselves in his or her place, and the story can serve as a sort of parable for our own journey in life.

Certainly we are likely to be able to identify with the feelings of puzzlement and depression which are evident in this story. Life is a strange mixture – sometimes beautiful, sometimes painful, and often bewildering. In this book we have already pondered on some of the experiences people find hard to bear – illness, disability, failure, injustice, bereavement, family strains and stresses, the whole assortment of negative pressures that characterise a society which has so evidently gone wrong. However, like the two on the way to Emmaus, we may find it is in our lowest moments that there comes onto the scene a stranger.

Cleopas and his companion did not recognise Jesus at first. All sorts of reasons have been suggested for this. They were travelling into the setting sun which might have impaired their vision. Their hearts were heavy and their eyes were probably fixed on the ground. There were certainly differences between Jesus' earthly body and his new risen body. But my guess is that mainly they did not recognise Jesus because he was the last person in the world they were expecting to see. The possibility of this event was not even remotely in their minds.

Jesus set about identifying himself – not only does he want to be with us, he wants us to know it. He struck up a conversation with the two travellers, asking questions and listening to their answers. They told him about their one-time trust in the friend they now thought was dead and gone. They told him about their feelings of hopelessness and bewilderment. Their darkness of soul seemed impenetrable.

For a moment the gentle stranger changed his approach.

It was time for some shock treatment. He told them they were dull of mind and slow of heart! As this rebuke jolted them out of their negativity, he spoke to them about deep and central scriptural truths. The Bible study, it seems, went on for quite some time: 'beginning with Moses and all the Prophets, he explained to them what was said in all the Scriptures concerning himself' (v27). He told them the Messiah had to suffer, but beyond that suffering lay unimaginable glory.

Time flew by, and suddenly they were home in Emmaus. For a moment it looked as though Jesus would leave them and continue his journey. But they held onto him, urging him to stay. It was late, they said, and would soon be dark. At their invitation he went inside. A meal was prepared, and they all sat down together. Jesus said a prayer of thanksgiving, broke the bread and gave it to them. And it was then, and only then, that 'their eyes were opened and they recognised him, and he disappeared from their sight' (v31).

At that moment 'Christ with us' became a personal reality for the two, and with this discovery came healing transformation. Their depression was replaced by new hope, their bewilderment by a new conviction, their torpor by new energy: 'They got up and returned at once to Jerusalem' (v33). The seven-mile walk seemed as nothing to them now. Their desire to get away, to be alone, was replaced by a desire for new closeness of relationship with those who loved the Lord Jesus. Together they shared what they knew to be true, and discovered that others too had experienced the wonder of the presence of the risen Christ. Then 'while they were still talking about this, Jesus himself stood among them and said to them, "Peace be with you" ' (v36).

And there we will leave them, enjoying Christ's presence and his peace, preparing themselves for the purpose and the power he would give them.

What about our own journey? Christ can be with us long before we know it. Our eyes may be closed by our pains and problems, or even sometimes by our success in life. How may we recognise him? Perhaps we may see him in the people we meet along life's way. Perhaps through the scriptures, though we may find that these take time to light up for us personally and we need the help of others.

'Jesus was recognised ... when he broke the bread' (v35), so if we are wise we won't neglect Christ's own service of Holy Communion in which bread is broken in his name. And we will seek the company of other Christians so that we may experience his presence together.

However, this has to be a personal as well as a corporate experience. You and I have to want Jesus to be our companion on our journey, and we have to tell him so. And we must be ready for the difference he will make with all its challenge and all its healing.

But enough of words! If you have already consciously started your journey with Jesus, you will know whether or not what I have been writing is true.

If you are still hesitating at the edge of the Christian experience, then this could be a crucial moment. You may like to look back to the prayer of response at the end of chapter nine. 'A journey of a thousand miles begins with a single step' – that prayer could be such a step. But if you have already taken it, here are two more prayers to take you further along your way. The first is a prayer of the Church in Wales (from *Prayers for Today's World*, Dick Williams [ed]):

•

I give my hands to you, Lord;
I offer the work I do;

I give my thoughts to you, Lord;
I give my words to you.

Give your hands to me, Lord;
   Let me have your joy;
Set me free to love, Lord;
   Lead me in your truth.

Give your words to me, Lord;
   Keep me close to you. Amen.

•

Lord, I am a countryman
   coming from my country to yours.
Teach me the laws of your country,
   its way of life,
   its spirit,
So that I may feel at home there.

William of Thierry

•

Remember – the Christ who is with us is the Saviour who loves to say 'Yes!'